*Economic Policy-Making and
Development in Brazil, 1947–1964*

Economic Policy-Making and Development in Brazil, 1947-1964

Nathaniel H. Leff

COLUMBIA UNIVERSITY

JOHN WILEY & SONS, INC.

NEW YORK · LONDON · SYDNEY · TORONTO

Written under the auspices of
The Center for International Affairs and
The Center for Studies in Education and Development
Harvard University

Library of Congress Catalog Card Number: 68-23924
SBN 471 52274 0
Printed in the United States of America

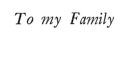

Acknowledgments

I am grateful to the many individuals and institutions who helped make this study possible. Adam Curle of Harvard University's Center for Studies in Education and Development and Edward S. Mason and Raymond Vernon of the Center for International Affairs supported the field work on which the study is based and provided the stimulating environment in which it was formulated. In Rio the Research Center operated jointly by the Economic Commission for Latin America (ECLA) and the Brazilian National Development Bank, under Dr. Aníbal Pinto, kindly made office facilities available to me. A similar courtesy was extended by the Brazilian Association for the Development of Basic Industry (ABDIB), under Dr. Jorge de Rezende, in São Paulo.

The Fundação Getúlio Vargas (particularly Dr. Julian Chacel, Dr. Isaac Kerstenetzky, Dr. Angelo de Souza, and Dr. Margaret Hanson Costa), and Dr. Eduardo Gomes, Jayr Dezolt, and Carlos Eduardo Mauro of the Research Division of SUMOC, the Brazilian Monetary Authority, were generous with statistical materials. Betty Mindlin Lafer rendered research assistance. I owe most, however, to the Brazilian businessmen, trade association officers, government officials, journalists, and politicians who in interviews supplied the bulk of the information on which the study is based.

John Plank, Paul N. Rosenstein-Rodan, and Kalman Silvert were very helpful in their suggestions and encouragement when the project was being formulated. The study also benefited greatly from my discussions with Albert Hirschman, Adam Curle, Richard Bird, David Felix, Donald Huddle, Joan Nelson, Celso Lafer, Richard Weisskopf, Octavio Dias Carneiro, Stefan Robock, and several members of the M.I.T. Political Science Department, in particular Lucian Pye, Myron Weiner, Harold Isaacs, and Robert Wood. I owe a very special debt to Frank Bonilla, R. S. Eckaus,

Daniel Lerner, and Thomas Skidmore for their many valuable comments on an early draft of the study. Douglas Chalmers, Christopher Clague, Samuel Huntington, Donald Keesing, Enrique Lerdau, Robert Packenham, Ronald Schneider, Gordon Smith, and Raymond Vernon read and provided many helpful suggestions on a later draft. Needless to say, none of these people bears responsibility for any of the study's deficiencies.

I am grateful to David Margolis and Jacob Dreyfus for their logistical support of the project. Robert Erwin, Carole Schwager, and Sanford Rose helped with their editorial skills. Margaret Thompson, Susan Hayward, Susan Lang and Wynelle Dale typed the manuscript with patience and care.

Finally, deepest thanks for her constant support and encouragement go to my wife, Judith.

Nathaniel H. Leff

New York City
December, 1967

Contents

Tables

Economic Policy-Making and
Development in Brazil, 1947–1964

CHAPTER I

Introduction

This is a study of the effects of politics on economic policy and economic development in Brazil.

Although the importance of public policy in promoting economic development is often emphasized, discussions of political conditions in many less-developed countries raise serious doubts concerning the possibilities for effective government action to promote economic development.[1] For example, governments may be simply unresponsive to the need for broad economic progress, either satisfied with the status quo or placing greater emphasis on other goals such as an aggrandizing foreign policy.

Another case may be called the "selfish elite" model. Here political pressures prevent the government from formulating or executing policies calculated to further development. Old or new elites control the machinery of government for their own purposes, standing in the way of policies that would jeopardize their own privileges, to the detriment of the country as a whole. In Latin America, and specifically in Brazil, such a picture of politics and economic policy-making has had widespread acceptance. Either the landowners, particularly the export sector—in Brazil, the coffee planters—or the growing industrialist class has been cast as the oligarchy constraining progressive policy-

---

[1] For a classical exposition of the structural conditions such as economic externalities, indivisibilities, and imperfect markets which, unless overcome by policy intervention, may prevent "natural" economic progress, see Paul N. Rosenstein-Rodan's "Problems of Industrialization of Eastern and South-Eastern Europe," *Economic Journal*, LIII (June–September 1943), and his "Notes on the Theory of the 'Big Push,'" in H. S. Ellis (ed.), *Economic Development for Latin America* (New York, 1961). For a general evaluation see Charles P. Kindleberger, *Economic Development* (New York, 1965), pp. 193–211.

making. Finally, another interpretation of politics and economic policy-making in Latin American countries such as Brazil may be called the "comic opera" case: for political reasons, the policy-making environment is unstable and chaotic, and it prevents purposeful action. As a result, policy is at best ineffectual and at worst seriously disruptive to the economy.

In this study we shall discuss the extent to which these models of policy-making and development are indeed relevant to postwar Brazil. It should be noted at the outset that prima facie the Brazilian experience hardly appears to support the hypothesis that politics and economic policy-making put a spoke in the wheel of economic development. Between 1947 and 1964, the period with which this book deals, Brazilian real output grew at an annual cumulative rate of almost 6 percent, based in great part on industrial development; this growth occurred despite some severe barriers such as low per capita income and an illiteracy rate over 50 percent. Although the country seems better suited for a discussion of the conditions that make a success story of economic development, the political interpretations cited are sometimes applied to Brazil.

In the first part of the study we shall consider what was done in specific areas of Brazilian economic policy. Although our focus is primarily analytical, some recounting of historical events is necessary before we can proceed to interpretation. As we shall see, the anecdotal and partial descriptions of these developments in Brazil are sometimes seriously misleading. Where the analysis of Brazilian politics given here diverges from conventional treatments, this is often because it is based on a very different empirical referent. At the same time, reconstruction of policy-making provides material for discussion of the political structure and the power relations within which decisions were made. The cases selected are well-suited for this purpose, for each focuses on a major factor in Brazilian politics. Tariff protection and coffee policy were key issues for the coffee planters, and those issues highlight their political position. Study of allocation decisions focuses on the place of the industrialists in Brazilian politics. Policy toward foreign investment illustrates the operation of one of the principal influences on governmental decision-making in Brazil—elite opinion. Export policy, finally, considers the role of doctrine in the formulation of Brazilian economic policy.

Part II of the study goes on to an overall discussion of the politics of economic policy in postwar Brazil. Here we deal with the structure within which interest articulation and aggregation have taken place, the power relations within the decision-making process, and the factors that have in fact determined policy. As this indicates, the study deals largely with "distributive" questions of politics. Specifically, who appears to control the state machine and in what direction is he driving it? Another aspect of political development that is largely omitted relates to the degree of social mobilization and the *aggregate* level of power in society: how powerful is the machine itself, regardless of who controls it.[2]

Before beginning our discussion, let us anticipate its major themes. In a political system where interest groups are powerful, they influence decision-making on specific issues that affect them by exerting controls on elected representatives and the executive. For example, industrialists may be expected to have an important voice in government allocation decisions relating to their industry. Broader groups such as socioeconomic classes would influence the overall framework within which interlocking issues are treated, and these would be dealt with in accordance with their broad interests and ideological perspective. Thus, export producers may be expected to influence the general strategy for dealing with the country's balance-of-payments and foreign-

---

[2] On the importance of this second question in political development, see Frederick W. Frey, "Political Development in Turkey," in Lucian Pye (ed.), *Communications and Political Development* (Princeton, N.J., 1963), pp. 302–303; Talcott Parsons, "The Distribution of Power in American Society," *World Politics* (October 1957). The focus largely on "distributive" aspects of politics is justified on the following grounds. First, expediency—to permit an adequate treatment of at least one important question concerning the impact of politics on economic development. Second, the question of who controls the policy-making machine and to what ends may well be more important for economic development. Although no one would claim that social and political mobilization during this period reached impressive levels in Brazil, a rapid rate of economic growth, supported by economic policy, was nonetheless possible. Indeed, after a point, a high level of aggregate power may well be dysfunctional for economic development. By the internal logic of social mobilization in such systems, much of the additional energy generated is devoted to noneconomic or anti-economic activities.

trade problems. I found very little evidence for such a pattern of strong interest group or class participation in Brazilian economic policy-making.

The general picture that emerges from the study is one in which the Brazilian government has had a substantial degree of autonomy from interest groups or socioeconomic class pressures in the making of economic policy. This autonomy resulted largely from a system of patronage politics which weakened "objective" political forces and transferred power to the politicians and the bureaucracy. Shielded from outside political pressures, they have been oriented largely by doctrine and by "public opinion"—mainly the views and information circulating among the political elite itself. Other important features of the policy-making process during this period were the influence of a modernizing nationalist ideology, and the power in economic issues of the career administrators in the civil service, who came to constitute a key group in economic policy formulation.

In going about the study, I drew upon the monograph literature and statistical data available on Brazil. Since little empirical material on decision-making in economic policy is published, I also relied heavily on personal interviews with the participants directly involved. These were conducted in Brazil between November 1963 and December 1964. The method followed was to seek out people who had participated in the formulation of policy in the case studies selected. This led me to eight cabinet ministers, mainly Finance Ministers, and to the principal economic advisors of two ministers who had since died. I also interviewed extensively senior government officials in the principal economic agencies: the Monetary Authority; the Development Bank; the Foreign Trade, and Rediscount Departments of the government-controlled Banco do Brasil; the National Tariff Council; the three public steel plants; and the "Executive Groups" established for sectoral planning in automobiles, shipbuilding, and heavy machinery. In the private sector, I interviewed the businessmen who had participated in these special planning and allocation agencies, and with the relevant interest groups—the São Paulo Federation of Coffee Planters, the São Paulo Federation of Industries, and three other important industrial trade associations. Interviews were also conducted with four of the largest private "economic groups" (similar to the Japanese *zaibatsu*) which have maintained an important political activity of their own.

Interviewing technique consisted of the formulation of open-ended questions which permitted respondents to answer freely and at length concerning the subjects raised. Questions focused on factual rather than interpretative material concerning the formulation of the policies and decisions in which interviewees had participated. Interviews were usually of relatively long duration, one to two hours, and with most participants more than one interview was conducted. This permitted sifting and cross-checking of the material. At the same time, respondents were almost all cooperative and, I believe, reliable in their narratives. Candor may have been facilitated by the fact that I dealt almost exclusively with historical rather than current events. Notes were taken in the course of the interviews, but a tape-recorder was not used. In the approach followed, material brought out in the first interviews served as the basis for subsequent sessions, until the topic was exhausted. This interviewing, pursued systematically with a wide variety of respondents, supplied much of the material on which this work is based. Since interviewees were promised anonymity, I have not named sources, but throughout the study data from a source not otherwise cited derive from interviews.

A final word on methodology. As mentioned, the focus of the work is analytical rather than descriptive. Histories of these events are available, and I have concentrated instead on the economic policy-making process.[3] This approach entails a loss in the detail and complexity of the picture. For example, I have treated the years 1947 to 1962 largely as one period. This view omits the nuances of the various subperiods, but it enables us to focus on the structural features which prove to be the essence of the story in Brazilian economic policy-making. Readers familiar with Brazil may also miss the to-and-fro maneuvers and the in-

---

[3] For detailed political histories of Brazil during this period, see José Maria Bello, *A History of Modern Brazil, 1889–1964* (Stanford, Cal., 1966), with a concluding chapter by Rollie E. Poppino; and Thomas E. Skidmore, *Politics in Brazil, 1930–1964: An Experiment in Democracy* (New York, 1967).

fighting that accompanied some government decision-making. However, our perspective does permit us to follow the main currents rather than the ebb and flow of day-to-day events toward some general conclusions on economic policy-making and development in Brazil.

Part 1

Economic Policy and
Brazilian Economic Development

CHAPTER 2

Protection and Coffee Policy

Early History of Brazilian Protection Policy

In 1844, with the expiration of a British treaty which had limited Brazil's freedom to impose tariffs, a 30 percent ad valorem duty was placed on most Brazilian imports. The measure was intended primarily to raise revenue for the federal government; but beginning in 1860 the tariff was revised persistently upward with avowedly protectionist aims. By 1874, the average rate on imports was approximately 40 percent, and in 1879, 50 percent, with a 60 percent rate on cotton textiles. In the early 1890's, the tariff was raised still further. After some reduction in 1897, the tariff was increased again in 1900 to put most rates at 50, 60, and 80 percent. Additional barriers to importation were imposed in 1905 and 1908 to give continuing high protection through the 1920's.[1]

In addition to the Treasury's support for higher tariffs as a source of revenue and as a means of reducing the country's balance-of-trade deficit, a protectionist policy received strong backing from several currents of elite opinion.[2] First, there was a nationalist desire to reduce the economy's "excessive" dependence on exports and vulnerability to foreign trade conditions. It was also emphasized that economic emancipation through increased self-sufficiency in primary products and manufactured

[1] On this whole long-term movement, see Nícia Vilela Luz, *A Luta pela Industrialização do Brasil*, (São Paulo, 1961), pp. 18, 36, 49, 111, 113, 118, 129, 170; and Stanley J. Stein, *The Brazilian Cotton Manufacture: Textile Enterprise in an Underdeveloped Area, 1850–1950* (Cambridge, Mass., 1957), pp. 81–85.

[2] In the late 1890's, tariffs accounted for approximately 70 percent of federal revenues. See Luz, p. 116, and regarding the balance of trade, p. 112.

goods was a prerequisite for political independence. Furthermore, industrialization was recommended as a means toward social and political modernization. Finally, there was strong political support for protection from several agricultural states, particularly Minas Gerais, which wanted to expand their production of foodstuffs and raw materials for the domestic market.[3]

The main opposition to protectionist policies came on doctrinal grounds, from free-traders who expounded the advantages of laissez faire and international specialization, and stressed the welfare costs of "artificial" industrialization. These were argued down by the protectionists, however, and even a professed liberal like Rui Barbosa accepted the economic advantages of protection for Brazil.[4] Importers, spokesmen for consumer interests, and the coffee planters (*fazendeiros*) also opposed the tariffs.[5] As the measures enacted indicate, however, they lacked the power to impose their preferences.

The opposition of the *fazendeiros* may have been mitigated by the fact that beginning in the last decades of the nineteenth century they were themselves enjoying a coffee boom that came simultaneously with the country's industrial expansion. When this threatened to collapse because of overproduction, the planters responded with their own economic policy measure, using the machinery of the São Paulo State government to restrict coffee supply in the first "valorization" programs.[6] These pro-

[3] Concerning these political currents, see Luz, pp. 71, 74–78, 100, 112, 116, 119, 126, 161, 165–166. Some of the contemporary flavor of the discussion is given in the following statement from the tariff debate of 1890, following Brazil's transformation from a constitutional empire to a republic. "[Without higher tariffs] the revolution would be a mere substitution of politicians . . . imposed by sterile principles, by abstract philosophy without the practical gain of economic and social renovation to improve the people's living conditions and progress . . . Even though a republic, Brazil will continue under the colonial system, merely an agricultural nation gathering raw materials for Europe, which returns them in manufactured form with an enormous profit, which supplies all manufactured products, everything necessary for life and comfort, in accordance with the economic system of which we, like the peoples of Asia and Africa, are victims . . ." This passage is cited in Luz, p. 100 (my translation).

[4] *Ibid.*, p. 161.

[5] *Ibid.*, pp. 114, 128.

[6] A careful study of coffee policy is provided in Antônio Delfim Netto, *O Problema do Café no Brasil*, (São Paulo, 1959). See also Celso Furtado, *The Economic Growth of Brazil*, translated by Ricardo de Aguiar and

grams indeed brought the coffee planters and the industrialists together on a basic policy issue, for they included a measure to intervene in the foreign-exchange market and lower the dollar-cruzeiro exchange-rate. Both groups wanted an undervalued rate: the planters to increase their earnings in domestic currency, the industrialists to raise the internal price of imports.[7]

High tariff protection continued in the first decades of the century, when the protectionists defeated a movement against industrialization and import substitution, which were blamed for the rising cost of living.[8] The pro-tariff forces were indeed strengthened by the country's rapid industrial development and by the political organization of the São Paulo industrialists.[9] By 1919, manufacturing interests so dominated the politics of this state that despite the protests of the coffee planters, the entire São Paulo congressional delegation voted against a proposal to lower import duties. The cotton textile manufacturers were particularly strong; to alleviate their condition of excess capacity and low returns in the 1920's, they were able to engineer a special tariff increase.[10] In 1930, however, the revolution led by Getúlio

Eric Drysdale (Berkeley, Calif., 1963), pp. 193–197, for a brief discussion of the first valorization programs.

[7] Luz, pp. 142–143, 179.

[8] The rapid increase in the money supply during these years was also relevant; and indeed the net effects of the Brazilian tariff are not always clear. Some data on the cotton textile industry, which has been studied intensively by Stanley Stein, cast doubt on the traditional interpretation which has contended that tariffs permitted internal prices well above world market levels and unusually high returns for the protected industries. Because of the size of internal market for some products and the large number of domestic producers, firms could not always set their prices at the world market level plus the tariff. Thus in 1914, Brazilian prices for a representative cotton product of mass consumption were reported at approximately half the price of imports with the tariff (Stein, pp. 105–106). In 1910, in the industry's "golden years," dividends in this industry were estimated to average 8 percent (Stein, p. 105).

[9] The complete economic history of these years has not yet been written, but a basic source is Warren Dean's "São Paulo's Industrial Elite, 1890–1960" (Ph.D. dissertation, University of Florida, 1964). Data on Brazilian development during this period are presented in Werner Baer, *Industrialization and Economic Development in Brazil* (Homewood, Ill., 1965), pp. 12–26, and my "Note on Brazilian Economic Development before 1939" (mimeo, 1967). On the political organization of the São Paulo industrialists, see Luz, pp. 122, 149.

[10] Stein, pp. 125–128.

Vargas brought important changes to Brazilian economic policy-making.

1930–1947

Although Getúlio takes his place in Brazilian history as a modernizer, his impact in this direction was confined largely to politics, and he did little during his first administration to promote industrialization.[11] Getúlio's economic views then apparently did not go beyond a personal leaning toward agrarianism and a concern for the welfare of the urban lower classes.[12] Apart from efforts to deal with coffee overproduction by restricting supply and destroying coffee inventories, economic policy measures in the 1930's were limited mainly to raising tariffs on agricultural products, social legislation for urban workers, restriction of foreign exploitation of Brazilian natural resources, and the first efforts at creation of the Volta Redonda steel mill. In the late 1930's, under the "Law of Similars," protection was accorded to some industrial products, but the effects of this legislation were often negated by administrative decisions, and there were long delays in the cumbersome process required for new products to be included in the protected list.[13] As late as 1940, Getúlio's presidential statement of economic goals reiterated the importance of agriculture, warned against the dangers of "excessive" urbanization, and made no mention of industrial development except in steel.[14]

The government's attitude toward industrialization was re-

[11] Cf. Dean's (*op. cit.*, pp. 128–133) emphasis on Getúlio's personal physiocratic inclinations and his hostility, during his first administration, toward the industrialists.

[12] In his memoirs, *A Aliança Liberal e a Revolução de 1930*, Vol. II (Rio de Janeiro, 1963), João Neves da Fontura, a close collaborator of Vargas, has also stressed Getúlio's economic xenophobia. Vargas also showed interest, pushed by the Brazilian military, in developing domestic steel production.

[13] In 1931 Getúlio did accede to the requests of the cotton textile manufacturers to limit output and competition by an embargo on textile machinery imports. This was apparently because he saw no other means of dealing with the economic crisis (Stein, pp. 140, 142). In 1938, however, when he had a staff memorandum which provided him with independent analysis of the industry's difficulties, Getúlio refused to renew the embargo (Stein, pp. 149–157).

[14] Dean, p. 130.

flected in its first major postwar economic policy decision—setting an overvalued dollar-cruzeiro exchange rate.[15] The policy was adopted despite the universal belief that it placed Brazilian industry in extreme jeopardy.[16] First, it was believed that some of the new industries developed during the war could not stand unrestricted competition with imports. Moreover, the disproportionate rise in the Brazilian price level as compared with the United States was thought to require a corresponding exchange-rate adjustment if the older domestic industries were to survive.[17] The government, however, continued in its previous orientation against "artificial" industrialization which might sacrifice consumer interests.[18] Brazilian policy here contrasts sharply with the measures adopted in similar circumstances by the Argentine government. In his efforts at economic modernization, Peron in 1945 refused to sacrifice the newly expanded domestic industries, and accorded them substantial tariff protection.[19]

The rationale for the Brazilian policy was fairly straight-

[15] The exchange rate was set at the 1939 level even though the internal price level had increased almost twice as much as prices in the United States, Brazil's principal foreign supplier.

[16] Since the early 1930's, tariffs had been levied as specific rather than ad valorem duties, and these had eroded to very low levels because of inflation. See Donald Huddle, "Furtado on Exchange Control and Economic Development: An Evaluation and Reinterpretation of the Brazilian Case," *Economic Development and Cultural Change*, XV, 271, nn. 14–15 (April 1967).

[17] Universal belief of the industrialists, their spokesmen, and the government concerning the ability of domestic manufacturing to withstand foreign competition without tariff protection turned out to be quite wrong. Industrial output expanded more rapidly in 1964–1947, when imports were available duty-free and at an overvalued exchange rate, than they had during the wartime period when overseas supply had been reduced because of shipping difficulties. Apparently Brazilian industry was much more able to compete with imports than was generally allowed for.

[18] Another policy measure strongly opposed by the industrialists was the government's 1946 prohibition of cotton textile exports. During the war years, Brazilian textile producers had developed a relatively large export market, exporting approximately 20 percent of their total production. Since international prices were higher than internal prices, the government prohibited exports in an effort to mitigate inflation and help the domestic consumer (Stein, pp. 175 ff.).

[19] Carlos Díaz-Alejandro, "Stages in Argentine Industrialization" (mimeo, 1965), p. 47.

forward, however. With the prospect of a substantial rise in coffee exports in the early postwar years and in the belief that coffee export receipts were maximized with an overvalued exchange rate, the government was attempting to secure a large inflow of imports at a relatively low domestic price. Competition from low-cost imports was also expected to inhibit inflationary price increases by domestic producers. These principles and preferences, however, were overturned by the balance-of-payments crisis of 1947, which evoked a policy response of import restriction.

Protection after 1947

Brazilian imports were at relatively high levels in 1946. By 1947, the exchange reserves accumulated during the war were exhausted, and demands for imports exceeded available foreign currency. As administrator of the foreign-exchange market and under pressure to equate the demand and supply of foreign currency, the government instituted quantitative restrictions on many imports.[20]

In this connection it is important to understand why the government did not deal with the balance-of-payments problem by another means—a straightforward devaluation, adjusting the exchange rate to clear the foreign-exchange market. (Indeed, with the 1947 devaluations in England and Europe, an area which supplied 47 percent of Brazilian imports in 1939 and 31 percent in 1949, maintaining the existing rate was tantamount to an exchange revaluation.) To control inflation, the government wanted cheap importation of certain commodities, such as wheat and petroleum, to whose price, it was believed, the cost of living was especially sensitive. Furthermore, the great lesson that Brazilian economic policy-makers had learned in the previous fifty years was that foreign demand for coffee was relatively inelastic with respect to price, and that consequently an overvalued exchange rate could be used to support world coffee prices. Since Brazil was the major world supplier, an across-the-board devaluation would only lower international coffee prices. Hence,

[20] For a detailed study of Brazilian policies during this period, see Donald Huddle, "Furtado on Exchange Control . . . ," *op. cit.*

although exchange depreciation would alleviate balance-of-payments pressures by an adverse movement of the terms of trade, it would also reduce the country's total imports.[21] In these conditions, the government understandably sought alternative policy measures.

The balance-of-payments problem was dealt with largely through quantitative restrictions on imports until October 1953, when the Monetary Authority instituted its famous Instruction 70. Protection continued, still based on foreign-currency shortage and the need for an allocation mechanism in the situation of excess demand that resulted from the decision not to clear the foreign-exchange market by means of a general devaluation. The licensing system, however, had led to several administrative scandals. Reacting to the movement of public opinion against corruption, a few high civil servants sought another means of equating the demand and supply of foreign exchange that would be less vulnerable to human failing. Their quest for what was conceived essentially as "an administrative problem" was to initiate a second phase—following the policy support for industrialization before and after the turn of the century—of Brazilian protection.

Instruction 70 established a five-compartment multiple-exchange system in which the government ranked imports according to their "essentiality." In each priority grouping, the government determined a base rate for an auction among importers to determine the exchange-rate premium (*ágio*) and the full cost for imports.[22] This premium now became an important

[21] The price elasticity of demand for coffee, Brazil's major export, has been estimated in the *F.A.O. Monthly Bulletin* (October 1954) at approximately 0.25. Moreover, since Brazil is the largest supplier, any devaluation of the cruzeiro which lowered the dollar price of coffee to foreign importers would probably be followed by retaliatory devaluation from other producers. Consequently, exchange-rate devaluation would not greatly increase the supply of foreign exchange and imports. See H. C. Wallich, *Monetary Problems of an Export Economy* (Cambridge, Mass., 1950), pp. 220–237, for a discussion of the balance-of-payments effects of devaluation under such conditions. The long-term effects of Brazilian exchange policy on coffee exports, and the effects of these measures on exportation of other commodities are discussed in Chapter 5 below.

[22] For a detailed discussion of the workings of the foreign-exchange auction system, see A. Kafka, "The Brazilian Exchange Auction," *Review of Economics and Statistics* (October 1956).

source of government revenue. Between 1954 and 1960, profits from the exchange auctions averaged 16 per cent of the federal government's tax revenues.

Not only did the Instruction raise the domestic cost of many imports, but it introduced important new criteria in applying the preferential exchange rates. Previously the major policy goal had been to control inflation by subsidizing imports of certain products considered crucial for price stability. Now, however, promotion of import substitution, in an effort to deal with the balance-of-payments problem, became more central to the focus of policy.

Behind this change lay the consideration that foreign-exchange shortage was now considered a long-term problem with which the government would have to contend.[23] As noted, the economic administrators rejected an across-the-board exchange depreciation because of its depressive effect on world coffee prices and total Brazilian imports. Protection, however, could be the functional equivalent of a selective devaluation. By raising the costs of imports in domestic currency, it would reduce demands for foreign exchange. And by increasing the price of imports relative to those of domestic producers, it would stimulate internal supply. This was seen as the best way of raising domestic consumption of manufactured products above the level permitted by export conditions. If domestic prices for these goods were sometimes higher than world market prices, this was only when converted at the official, overvalued exchange rate. The higher price permitted import-substituting industries, however, was only a recognition that the equilibrium exchange rate and the real cost of additional imports in fact stood considerably higher than that implied by the official rate.

The new system also put the de facto protection given many industrial products on a much firmer institutional basis. Protection was no longer considered as an emergency response to a transitory balance-of-payments crisis but was looked upon as an established institution for dealing with a long-term problem. The selection of priorities for importation also constituted a more conscious effort to develop import substitution of manufactured

[23] Chapter 5 discusses the reasons why export promotion was not adopted as a policy response to the balance-of-payments problem.

products. Hence Instruction 70 proved to be a major milestone in Brazilian protection and policy support for industrialization.

The multiple exchange-rate system established by Instruction 70 was the major instrument of protection until 1956–1957, when tariff legislation was passed. The institutional basis of protection was changed for several reasons. The international economic agencies, the International Monetary Fund (IMF) and the General Agreement on Trade and Tariffs (GATT), were pressing the government to end the multiple exchange-rate system. The number of exchange categories was now reduced from five to two. In addition, the legislature had followed the pro-industrialization climate of opinion in the press and among the younger administrators in the economic agencies to the point where congressional support for tariff legislation could now be attained.

The new legislation also introduced an institutional innovation, the National Tariff Council. This body was composed of representatives of the government economic agencies—the foreign-exchange and monetary authorities and the National Development Bank—and of industrial, import, and agricultural interest groups. Although pressure-group representation was institutionalized in the new arrangement, testimony of participants agrees that the government administrators usually dominated the Council's decisions.[24] Their position, in turn, was generally dictated by the all-pervading desire to relieve pressure on the balance of payments.[25]

There was disagreement within the Council, for example, when new industries producing intermediate products were established. These commodities had previously been imported at a low exchange and tariff rate because of their "essentiality" as inputs to other industries. With development of domestic production, however, they were placed on the higher import-cost list. Although this usually provoked opposition from client industries, the government always pointed out that the chronic

---

[24] The material that follows is based on interviews with past members of the Council.
[25] Cf. Furtado, *Economic Growth of Brazil*, and Werner Baer, *Industrialization and Economic Development in Brazil* (Homewood, Ill., 1965), pp. 48–61, for a similar interpretation of Brazilian protection policy during this period.

foreign-exchange shortage gave it no choice but to accept any effort at import substitution that would lessen the demand for imports.[26] Given the existence of the balance-of-payments deficit as a persistent, high-priority problem for which they perceived no alternative policy response, opponents had no choice but to accept the government's decisions.

The importance of foreign-exchange shortage in determining protection policy can be seen in the government's treatment of equipment imports which were financed by overseas supplier credits or by foreign private investors. Throughout the 1950's the government accorded preferential exchange-rate treatment and suspended tariffs on such imports,[27] which amounted to a very large portion—approximately 80 percent between 1955 and 1960—of all Brazilian equipment imports.[28] Such investment goods were welcomed by the government because of their contribution to capital formation and the domestic production of other goods pressing on the import list. Moreover, since these imports brought their own foreign-exchange supply, they were not considered an additional pressure on the balance of payments. Under these conditions, the government turned a deaf ear to the domestic equipment industry's petitions for protection.

By the early 1960's, however, the debt service and profit-remission charges created by this capital inflow began to weigh heavily on the balance of payments.[29] Believing that the best way to reduce future foreign-exchange demands for capital

[26] Government policy throughout this period was based on the assumption, which was regarded as self-evident, that domestic production of goods previously imported would reduce foreign-exchange demands. The effect of income creation in generating demands for new imports was generally neglected. For a discussion of the balance-of-payments effects of import sustitution in Brazil, see a paper by myself and Antônio Delfim Netto, "Import Substitution, Foreign Investment, and International Disequilibrium in Brazil," *Journal of Development Studies* (April 1966).

[27] Exemption from tariffs for equipment imports financed by foreign suppliers was provided in special legislation and in administrative rulings by the National Tariff Council. This is discussed in Chapter 6 of my study *The Brazilian Capital Goods Industry* (Cambridge, Mass., 1968). Tariff exemption for direct foreign investors, who accounted for some 20% of all foreign capital inflow, was provided in SUMOC Instruction 113. This is discussed in Chapter 4 below.

[28] Computed from data supplied by the Research Division of SUMOC (the Brazilian Monetary Authority).

[29] The following data indicate the sharp rise of capital charges as a percentage of all foreign-exchange payments in the Brazilian international

charges lay in limiting present imports of foreign-financed equipment, the government applied severe restrictions against such imports. Here balance-of-payments considerations outweighed first the petitions of the domestic capital goods industry against imports, and subsequently the pressure of firms attempting to import foreign-financed equipment.

Some unspoken attitudes of the policy-makers were another important feature of the decision process. The possibility of dealing with the balance-of-payments problem by stabilizing income and consumption at the levels dictated by current export receipts was apparently never seriously considered. This activist orientation was a basic feature of the milieu within which economic policy was framed throughout this period. Similarly, the decision to deal with the balance-of-payments problem by import substitution rather than, or even concomitantly with, export expansion stemmed from another unspoken but basic feature of policy-making. This crucial orientation was taken so much for granted by almost all participants that there was hardly any perception that an alternative policy response existed.

We should also note the extent of the government's freedom of action in making policy. The major changes in economic policy—the institution in 1947 of import licensing and in 1953, of a multiple exchange-rate system—were decided by executive order. The items selected and the criteria applied for the various import priorities were also determined by discretionary administrative decision. Even with the tariff legislation of 1956–1957 and the institutionalization of interest-group access, the government retained its discretion in administering import regulation.

This autonomy is especially noteworthy because government policies toward protection went directly against the orientation of a major actor in Brazilian politics: the export sector, particularly the coffee interests. Our discussion here contrasts with interpretations of Brazilian politics which emphasize the predominance of the *fazendeiros*.[30] Their inability to veto public policy

accounts: 1948–1952, 4.7 percent; 1956–1960, 15.3 percent; 1961–1963, 24.0 percent. Computed from material in "Auge y Declinación del Proceso de Sustitución de los Importaciones en el Brasil," *Boletín Económico de América Latina*, IX (March 1964), Table 3; and from *Boletim da Sumoc*, 1964.

[30] The latter interpretation is of course not held universally. Stein (*op. cit.*, pp. 125–126, 135), for example, has dated the *fazendeiros*' political eclipse to the 1920's, even earlier than suggested below.

in the area of protection is especially noteworthy, for they had always opposed government support for industrialization, which they believed would entail a rise in price and deterioration in quality of the manufactured goods they purchased. This case then raises the issue of the extent of the coffee planters' power in determining Brazilian economic policy. We turn now to a more detailed discussion of this question.

The Coffee Planters and Brazilian Coffee Policy

The coffee sector's principal alternative to prevent an adverse movement of its terms of trade (i.e., the relative price of coffee and industrial products) would have lain in a policy of "parity," by which the government would have maintained an internal price ratio favorable to the sector. This was the course followed,

TABLE 1.   *Relative Price Ratio of Prices Paid to Coffee Exporters and Prices of Industrial Products in Brazil, 1950–1964*

(A) Year	(B) Cruzeiro Price Paid by the Government to Coffee Exporters (Index)	(C) Industrial Prices (Index)	(D) Relative Prices (B/C)
1950	100	100	100
1951	110	118	93
1952	113	128	88
1953	130	147	88
1954	212	194	109
1955	207	221	94
1956	209	274	76
1957	201	321	63
1958	183	375	49
1959	268	538	50
1960	329	665	50
1961	433	947	46
1962	577	1372	42
1963	892	2516	37
1964	2522	4620	55

Source. Columns (B) and (C) are from indices 105 and 49 of *Conjuntura Econômica.* (B) was divided by (C) to obtain the relative price ratio. The year 1950 is used as a base because it was a good year for coffee and might well serve as a "golden age" on which to base parity calculations.

for example, by politically powerful producers of some agricultural products in the United States when they were faced with a
similar deterioration of their market prices. The instrument for
such a policy was readily available in Brazil if the coffee sector
had been strong enough to carry it. The government has controlled coffee prices and could easily have adjusted them to keep

TABLE 2. *Relative Price Ratio of Coffee and of Other Agricultural
Commodities in Brazil, 1950–1964*

(A) Year	(B) Cruzeiro Price Paid by the Government to Coffee Exporters (Index)	(C) Agricultural Price Index Excluding Coffee (Index)	(D) Relative Prices (B/C)
1950	100	100	100
1951	110	123	91
1952	113	144	78
1953	130	170	77
1954	212	200	106
1955	207	249	91
1956	209	299	71
1957	201	332	61
1958	183	370	50
1959	268	527	69
1960	329	741	44
1961	433	1024	42
1962	577	1620	37
1963	892	2718	33
1964	2522	4889	55

Source. Columns (B) and (C) are from indices 105 and 48 of *Conjuntura
Econômica.* (B) was divided by (C) to obtain the relative price ratio.

pace with or exceed industrial price rises. As Table 1 shows,
however, this did not occur. On the contrary, the government
held down the prices paid to coffee exporters, adjusting them
only with a lag in the rise of industrial prices. Table 2 indicates
that the price paid coffee exporters also fell significantly behind
prices of other agricultural commodities.[31] Far from receiving a

[31] Available data also permit us to compare the evolution of internal coffee
prices with the prices of individual agricultural commodities in São Paulo

subsidy to enable their prices to increase more rapidly than other prices or even from getting "parity" treatment enabling them merely to keep pace, the coffee planters had the internal terms of trade turned aggressively against them.

Although the internal prices paid for coffee hardly appear to be evidence of the *fazendeiros'* political hegemony, we should also consider the broader question of the government's maintaining a guaranteed market for coffee to see what light this sheds on reciprocal power relations. Coffee policy since the 1930's has shown important differences from the period 1906 to 1930, when intervention was conducted unambiguously for the planters' special interests. By contrast, in the modern period, when the interests of the government and the export sector in coffee policy have diverged, the government has made its wishes prevail.

In 1931 the federal government took charge of Brazilian coffee policy, which had previously been conducted by São Paulo State. The change in administrative locus came together with an important shift in Brazilian politics. Whereas the *fazendeiros* had exercised considerable influence in São Paulo, the federal administration under Getúlio Vargas had come to power in armed rebellion against the previous system of Brazilian politics, in which the coffee elite had played a leading role.[32]

State during this period. These price indices, computed in constant cruzeiros on a 1948-1952 base, show the following results for 1958-1959:

Rice	131
Beans	110
Corn	106
Meat	96
Sugar	83
Coffee	57

The data are from ECLA-FAO, *El Café en América Latina*, Vol. II, *Estado de São Paulo*, (Mexico City, 1960), Pt. I., p. 101.

[32] In the months following the Wall Street Crash of October 1929 and preceding the Vargas Revolution of 1930, the situation of Brazilian coffee worsened drastically. International prices fell at the same time as foreign loans to continue the coffee-retention program were cut off. The Brazilian federal government refused, however, to accede to the requests of the coffee planters to respond either with credits to enable them to hold inventories or with a moratorium on their debts. (See João Neves da Fontura, pp. 223-237.) This experience supports Stanley Stein's suggestion, cited in n. 30, that even in the regime preceding the Vargas Revolution,

Under the federal government's coffee-retention policy, the government has purchased coffee and held stocks in years when the world market would not absorb Brazilian coffee exports at desired prices. This policy developed out of the fall of coffee prices following the 1929 Depression and the inability of the private sector or of São Paulo State to hold the enormous inventories which had accumulated to prevent even lower prices.[33] The planters' interests have been served by a stable market, but the government's intervention reflects its effort to act as a monopolist in the international coffee market, restricting supply in order to increase the economy's foreign-exchange earnings. In a certain measure these two goals—stabilizing planter income and maximizing the country's export receipts from coffee—have coincided. In some respects, however, the interests of the planters and the government have diverged significantly.

The planters, for example, have traditionally wanted an *undervalued* dollar-cruzeiro exchange rate, to raise their cruzeiro earnings for a given world market price. Thus one of the major provisions of the 1906 "valorization" program was an intervention in the foreign-exchange market to lower the exchange rate. This involved a devaluation of approximately 30 percent—in the midst of rapidly growing exports—a move that was considered open exploitation of other consumer interests.[34] Coffee policy in the modern period, however, has *overvalued* the exchange rate, in an effort to raise international coffee prices and maximize foreign-exchange receipts for the economy as a whole rather than cruzeiro earnings for the coffee planters.[35]

Furthermore, the government has used its control of the foreign-exchange market to pay coffee producers much less than it received for their coffee exports on the world market. Under the so-called "exchange confiscation," coffee exporters have had

the federal government was not as subservient to the planters as has sometimes been suggested.

[33] See Netto, pp. 129–146, for a discussion of coffee policy during this period.

[34] See J. Pandiá Calógeras, *A Política Monetária do Brasil*, (São Paulo, 1960), pp. 435–464.

[35] On the different goals of exchange-rate policy in these two periods, see Netto, 78 ff.

to convert their dollar earnings at an exchange rate considerably lower than the rates paid by importers.[36] The difference between the Foreign Exchange Authority's two rates constituted a severe export tax on the planters. Data on the extent of this taxation are available from 1954, as presented in Table 3. The gov-

TABLE 3. *Taxation of Coffee Exports, 1954-1963*

Year	Export Taxation as a Percentage of the Total Value of Coffee Exports
1954	23%
1955	17
1956	37
1957	33
1958	48
1959	42
1960	39
1961	46
1962	55
1963	53

Source. From data supplied by the Research Division of SUMOC, this table was calculated by the following procedures. The dollar value of annual coffee exports was converted to cruzeiros by the annual average import exchange-rate, that is, cruzeiro cost of all imports divided by their dollar cost. This in turn was compared with the cruzeiro amount which the government paid to the coffee exporters. These computations and further details are presented in Table 21 of the Statistical Appendix.

ernment was able to appropriate for itself a good part, exceeding 50 percent in some years, of the value of coffee exports.[37] As

[36] The "exchange confiscation" originated in the late 1930's as a small margin instituted in the *Banco do Brasil's* foreign-exchange transactions, but it became an important source of government revenue only in the 1950's. According to the men who initiated the program, it was intended as a simpler and politically less visible device for milking the coffee planters than a more extensive intervention, which Vargas had suggested.

[37] The data of Table 3 overstate the extent of taxation because in some years, the government bought more coffee than it could sell at desired prices. Adding these costs would reduce the taxation percentage, and in some years of low export values would turn it negative, as indicated in Table 22 of the Statistical Appendix. However, in addition to their opposition, noted below, to the government's general coffee policy, the coffee

Table 4 indicates, this percentage was considerably higher than

TABLE 4. *Prices Received by Planters in Major Coffee-Producing Countries as a Percentage of Export Prices, 1965*

Country	Percent
Angola	93
Ethiopia	80
Guatemala	74
El Salvador	73
Colombia	72
Mexico	65
Brazil	31

Source. Peter Knight, "The Critical Coffee Sector in Brazil" (mimeo, Stanford University, 1966), p. 8. Knight drew upon *Annual Coffee Statistics, 1965,* Tables REV-5, EQ-2, and upon U.S. Department of State Agricultural Attaché reports.

the share which governments of other coffee-exporting countries extracted from their producers.

In the course of the 1950's, the coffee planters protested vigorously against this taxation, rallying behind the slogan of a "single exchange rate" (*taxa única*), according to which their dollar earnings would be converted at the same (much higher) rate that applied to imports.[38] Indeed, since the early 1950's, the

planters maintained that in view of the importance of coffee exports to the Brazilian economy, the burden of the retention program should be borne by society as a whole and not by themselves. Moreover, the value of the government's gains in years of positive taxation, was much greater than its losses in the years of negative taxation. First, the percentage of the gains, averaging 19 percent, was considerably larger than the percentage of the losses, which averaged 7 percent. The losses also came in years of small export values, so that the magnitudes were much less than those of the government's gains, which occurred in years of much higher absolute exports. If we bear in mind the data of Tables 1 and 2, which show the sharp rise in the relative price of manufactured goods and of other agricultural products—costs which also influenced the *fazendeiros*' real income— the general picture of the planters being treated harshly rather than favored by government policy appears valid.
[38] The coffee planters' call for a single exchange rate coincided with the International Monetary Fund's general opposition to multiple exchange-rate systems and its repeated demand for exchange-rate "consolidation" ac-

São Paulo coffee-planters' association had been calling for a radical revision in the government's entire policy toward coffee. Reacting to the sharp decline in Brazil's share of the world coffee market, they proposed an export policy which would lower international coffee prices, drive out other—presumably higher-cost—producers, and greatly increase the volume of Brazil's coffee exports.[39] Their petitions were rejected, however, and the existing policy was continued.[40] To add to the high-handed treatment of the coffee sector, Instruction 70, which elaborated the multiple exchange-rate system, had stipulated that any surplus accruing from coffee exports should be redistributed to the planters through a Fund for the Modernization of Agriculture. The surplus proved far greater than anyone foresaw, but the Fund was never constituted, and the government simply appropriated these resources.

This treatment of the coffee planters in relative prices and in export taxation hardly suggests that they have enjoyed the political hegemony attributed to the export sector in many under-developed countries.[41] Reflecting their sense of political weakness and frustration, the planters have since the late 1940's expressed bitter resentment against the "bureaucratic oligarchies" and "city experts" (*técnicos do asfalto*) formulating coffee policy.[42] In Chapter 8 we will discuss the government administrators (*técnicos*) who played this important role, but we

companied by devaluation. As a result, the planters and the IMF have appeared as political allies pressing the same demand on the government. This was damaging for both parties politically. The odium which Brazilian elite opinion attached to each redounded to the discredit of the other. Their association appeared to confirm the interpretation that they were both interested in maintaining Brazil as a colonial, export economy.

[39] See the speeches by Salvio de Almeida Prado, head of the São Paulo Planters' Organization during the late 1940's and the 1950's: *Dez Anos na Política do Café*, (São Paulo, 1956), pp. 208–215.

[40] SUMOC Instruction 204 of 1961 did reduce the number of exchange rates and make some progress toward a single, devalued rate. This was hardly a victory for the planters, however, for the same measure institutionalized the "exchange confiscation," which was now recognized formally as the "contribution quota."

[41] Another study of Brazilian economic policy in this period comes to similar conclusions. See "Fifteen Years of Economic Policy in Brazil," *Economic Bulletin for Latin America*, IX, 156 (November 1964).

[42] See e.g., *Dez Anos na Política do Café*, pp. 240–242.

should note their appearance here as objects of the planters' hostility.

Displaced from their previous position of a major participant in the decision-making process, the planters have been able only to criticize the government for its "ignorance of coffee conditions" and its "unwillingness to believe qualified informants"—such as the agricultural interest groups—as a result of which successive administrations were "completely out of touch with the real situation." [43] In the one instance in which they tried to raise the level of their pressure on the government, with a (motorized) march on the Capitol in 1958, the *fazendeiros* were so isolated politically that the government simply dispatched troops to disband them and sent them home, grievances unsatisfied.

This distance from the seats of power continued through the 1950's, as the planters were reduced to the position of outsiders conspiring against the ongoing system. Indeed, they were so alienated from the rest of Brazilian politics that they were not even on close terms with the other conspirators! A final indication of the planters' political decline came after the movement of April 1964, in which the military, backed by conservative and center groups, deposed President João Goulart. The coffee groups expected a sympathetic hearing from the new regime, for they had been among Goulart's most vigorous opponents. Their power had been so greatly overshadowed, and Brazilian coffee policy so determined by other considerations, however, that the new regime's orientation was no closer to their wishes than that of preceding governments. Within weeks after April 1964, the planters' representatives were voicing violent criticism of the Castello Branco regime in interviews with *Última Hora*, one of the most virulent opposition newspapers.

Causes of the Planters' Political Decline

The process by which the coffee planters were displaced as a dominant political elite in a relatively short period and with a minimum of bloodshed is clearly an important subject that merits detailed treatment. Although such a project is outside the scope of this book, several points can be noted.

[43] *Ibid.*, pp. 225, 215.

First, the planters were dealt an enormous economic and psychological blow by the 1929 coffee crisis. On top of this came the Vargas Revolution of 1930 and the military failure of the São Paulo Rebellion of 1932, which the *fazendeiros* supported. They never again recovered their *élan*. The Revolution of 1930 instituted a new political era similar, in some respects, to the changes introduced by Peron in Argentina. A group which included some young modernizers seized power, with support from the military, and initiated important changes in the previous political system. At the same time, accelerated industrialization and urbanization increased the number of voters beyond control of the older rural political machines and added new potential centers of power in the industrialists and urban workers. Not only did these new political forces outflank the export sector, but they also introduced a new complexity to Brazilian politics. Too many significant actors were now involved for issues to be resolved through the simple domination of a major group.

The conflict between modern urban forces and the coffee planters also had an important structural feature which gave rise to a certain "threshold" effect. Both coffee planting and manufacturing were concentrated in the same region, São Paulo. Consequently, once the balance of power within this state had shifted, a "tipping" phenomenon occurred, in which the political weight of the whole region was thrown behind the winning modern sector. In the relatively short period between the first decade of the century and the middle 1940's, São Paulo State, with its enormous weight within Brazilian politics, switched from the bastion of coffee to the support of industrial interests in the national arena. The contrast here is with a situation such as that of the United States, where the export sector-manufacturing conflict was not concentrated within a single region. Hence, even when defeated on the national scene, the export sector in the United States could muster the support of its region and maintain a creditable showing in national politics rather than undergo a relatively sudden eclipse.[44]

[44] It has sometimes been suggested that the tensions accompanying the political decline of the planters were mitigated because the traditional coffee elite also had extensive interests in the emerging industrial sector. I found little support for such a contention, and neither did Warren Dean

We can also note some other features of the planters' political decline. The *fazendeiros* never adapted their political style and techniques to the new age, particularly as regards mobilization of support among the intelligentsia and elite opinion.[45] In particular, they never related their claims to anything broader than the traditional importance of coffee in the economy. In the context of modernizing Brazilian ideology, however, this was something everyone else wanted to forget; indeed, its modification was one of the central goals of Brazilian economic policy. Moreover, their petitions usually did not involve anything more than the price of coffee. They rarely related these claims effectively in a broad program dealing with the other economic problems with which the government had to contend: the balance of payments, inflation, employment for a growing population. Consequently, they were at a severe tactical disadvantage when the government rejected their requests because of alleged requirements in other policy areas.

Coming together with these other features, coffee policy was itself a powerful instrument for subjugating the coffee sector to the government's leadership. Because the government dominated the internal coffee market, it was always able to quiet the planters' opposition by punitive action or threatened manipulation of its extensive economic instruments in price, credit, or storage policy.[46]

in his previously cited dissertation. Dean identified three early sources of entrepreneurship and capital in São Paulo's industrial development: coffee planters, importers, and immigrants. The latter two greatly overshadowed the importance of the coffee planters (pp. 13, 26, 149). Furthermore, the percentage of planter-industrialists within the entire *planter* class—which is the relevant consideration for the present question—was very small. Stanley Stein, *op. cit.*, also makes no mention of an extensive movement from coffee to textiles, either in the industry's early years or in the 1920's and 1930's. The number of coffee families who transferred a portion of their assets to the new industrial sector does not greatly exceed the very few (e.g., Villares, Vidigal) who are usually cited as "examples" of such behavior. To the extent that resources were transferred from coffee to industry, this occurred through fiscal policy, the "exchange confiscation" tax, which, as seen in Chapter 3, the government allocated largely to *public* sector corporations.

[45] In this and subsequent chapters, reference is often made to elite opinion and public opinion. These are discussed in detail in Chapter 8.

[46] A similar development seems also to have occurred with the national government's control of sugar production. The Brazilian Institute of Sugar and Alcohol (Instituto de Alcool e Açucar) was founded in the 1930's in an

The Inefficiencies of Brazilian Coffee Policy

Although the government had the power to control the *fazendeiros* and implement policy as it chose, even within the framework of an oligopolistic export strategy Brazilian coffee policy has shown some serious deficiencies.[47] Because of poor information and technical analysis within the policy-making process, the retention policy was operated inefficiently and entailed large, unnecessary costs.

As a consequence of Brazil's export policy, the volume of Brazilian coffee exports was practically stable during the postwar period. Internal coffee production, however, doubled.[48] This large increase in production went to the government-held coffee inventories. As Table 5 indicates, these constituted 1 to 2 percent of Brazilian GNP during the late 1950's. The waste in resources is even more impressive if we realize that these additions to inventories amounted to between 5 and 10 percent of aggregate Brazilian savings and gross investment during these years.

As noted earlier, the government set prices for coffee exporters which were only a fraction of export values. These fell rapidly behind the rise in the prices of industrial products and of other agricultural commodities as well. Internal prices were low enough to force marginal producers out of coffee; the share of coffee in the agricultural output of São Paulo State fell 20 percent during the 1950's.[49] Nevertheless, the internal price for

effort to protect local sugar producers, at that time largely in the Northeast, from the price declines of the Depression. Through its control of prices, credit and marketing, the government was able to neutralize opposition of the Northeast planters to the major policy decision affecting the industry during the 1940's and 1950's—the allocation of the increment of Brazilian sugar production to new producers in the Center-South region. By 1963–1964, the Center-South produced approximately 62 per-cent of all Brazilian sugar, as compared with 37 per-cent for the Northeast. São Paulo State alone produced almost as much sugar as the entire Northeast region, and twice as much as the State of Pernambuco, the traditional leader in sugar production. These data are from *Anuário Estatístico—1966*, (Rio de Janeiro, 1967).

[47] The export strategy itself is discussed in Chapter 5.
[48] Data are from Baer, pp. 277, 258.
[49] ECLA-FAO, *El Café en América Latina*, Vol. II, *Estado de São Paulo* (Mexico City, 1960), Pt. I, pp. 86–106, especially p. 94.

TABLE 5. *Annual Increase in Government Coffee Inventories as a Percentage of Brazilian GNP, 1957–1962*

Year	Percent
1957	1.1
1958	2.1
1959	2.8
1960	2.1
1961	0.9
1962	2.0

Source. "Fifteen Years of Economic Policy in Brazil," *Economic Bulletin for Latin America,* IX (November 1964), p. 183.

coffee still constituted an incentive sufficient to stimulate substantial overproduction.

The government's prices were set in an *ad hoc* manner, extracting from the planters an amount that was a sizable fraction of previous conventional prices. In light of the high tax levied, this was thought to be considerable squeezing of the producers. Policy-makers were not aware, however, that during this period the costs of coffee production were falling sharply because of the opening of more fertile regions in Paraná, and because of the development and rapid diffusion of new, more productive coffee strains (particularly the *Mundo Novo*).[50] Consequently even with taxes which were high when considered in relation to *previous* prices and costs, the government's price to the exporters was still sufficient to generate a large expansion of production.

The problem was further compounded by technical difficulties which prevented an easy adjustment to overproduction. Because of the coffee tree's four to five year gestation period, the large surpluses reached the market only after producers had responded to prices offered five years earlier. Although relative prices and taxation moved increasingly against coffee during the

[50] *Ibid.,* pp. 28–30.

1950's, the new coffee plantations had been predicated upon earlier conditions. Not only was a lag involved, but the supply curve also had a significant kink over a large range of prices. Once producers had incurred the high fixed costs of planting new trees, supply was inelastic unless prices fell so drastically that they were below the planters' variable costs—a relatively small fraction of full average cost. Policy-makers, however, were reluctant to reduce prices so sharply. They feared the unforseeable long-term consequences of disrupting the production of a commodity that accounted for more than half of the country's foreign-exchange earnings.

This experience emphasizes the obvious point that political control is not sufficient to ensure the formulation of effective economic policy. Policy-makers must also have adequate information on which to base their actions, while technical rigidities and uncertainties may also present difficulties.

Conclusions

In this chapter we have noted several important features of Brazilian economic policy-making. First, the conditions in which protection was implemented during the nineteenth century are worth noting. Tariffs were provided largely in response to modernizing and nationalist currents in elite opinion and antedated the emergence of a strong industrialist class. Furthermore, there was no conflict between the advocates of agricultural and industrial development, for generous tariffs were established at the same time for both types of products. There was also no frontal clash between policies for export expansion and industrialization; rather, the government intervened with policy measures for both groups. Indeed, the coffee planters and the industrialists came together in their support for a measure of common interest—undervaluation of the exchange rate. Thus some of the "classical" political conflicts concerning the pattern of Brazil's economic development were largely avoided.

We have also noted the interventionist and activist orientation of Brazilian economic policy well before the economic crisis of the 1930's. Apart from the tariff legislation, a marked departure from laissez faire occurred with the government's direct interventions to support the industrial firms hurt by the credit squeeze of the middle 1890's.[51] The valorization programs demonstrate the Brazilians' activist orientation, for they were among the few primary producers that attempted to intervene in the market to better their economic position. As these examples indicate, there are also no grounds for attributing to the Brazilian political elite an undue deference to "doctrines developed in the advanced countries but inappropriate for Brazil." The frequent government budget deficits, the rapid increase in the money supply, and the persistent inflation in the nineteenth and early twentieth centuries are another indication of how little Brazilian governments actually let themselves be influenced by "orthodox" views.[52] As we will see in subsequent chapters, Brazilian policy-makers may not always have acted with complete wisdom, but there are no grounds for charging them either with passivity or with doctrinaire adherence to "imported theories."

Our discussion also indicates that Brazilian decision-makers were able to formulate and implement economic policy with a fair degree of autonomy from political pressures. In its major economic policy action for the postwar period, the government set an overvalued exchange rate—without, moreover, granting protection to the domestic industries that were expected to be out-competed by a flood of imports. Brazilian industrialists were unable to stop these measures aimed directly at what they had always considered their primary policy goal, protection. Subsequent balance-of-payments pressures forced the government into a policy of protection and support for import-substituting industrialization. Here the government was able politically to proceed with measures the coffee planters had long opposed. The treatment accorded the planters in the areas of relative prices and export taxation indicated further that the export sector has no longer had a dominant position in Brazilian politics.

With the expansion of the manufacturing sector in the 1950's, some writers have suggested that industrial interests

[51] Luz, pp. 101–107.
[52] For data on monetary and fiscal policy before 1910, see Calógeras, *A Política Monetária do Brasil*. Data on the federal government deficits, on increases in the money supply, and on price inflation since 1900 are presented in Baer, pp. 289–290, 287, 300–301.

dominated Brazilian economic policy-making.[53] Because of the chronic balance-of-payments problem and the commitment to import-substituting industrialization, interests of the government and of the industrialists were largely in harmony over protection. In Chapter 3, however, we will examine economic policy-making *within* the context of the industrialization effort. Here ample scope for political conflict did exist, and this case provides further material for judging where decisive power in Brazilian economic policy-making lay.

[53] See, e.g., "Fifteen Years of Economic Policy in Brazil," p. 190.

CHAPTER 3

Allocation Policy

The Brazilian government has had the power to play an extensive role in the economy. In addition to the fiscal, monetary, and regulatory activities carried on by most governments, it has exercised many direct economic controls and maintained a wide range of production and investment activities. An ECLA study of Brazilian economic policy presents this picture:

> Brazil's public sector owns . . . the country's maritime . . . rail transport facilities and its installations for the production of petroleum . . . controls most of the steel-making sector, and is rapidly becoming the principal producer of electric energy. It . . . markets a considerable proportion of the exportable production; it is also the principal iron ore producer and exporter. It exercises direct . . . control over the exchange market. . . .
> It constitutes . . . the major commercial banking enterprise since it accounts for about 35 percent of the general credit extended to the private sector through the *Banco do Brasil,* and most of the agricultural credit . . . Through other specialized financial agencies it grants the whole of cooperative credit and long-term financing. It establishes wages, interest rates, rents, and staple commodity prices. It sets minimum agricultural prices and is beginning to . . . operate a large-scale storage and marketing system for agricultural commodities. . . . It determines the composition of private investment and intervenes in the capital market.[1]

A consideration of how the government used these powers in the allocation of resources is especially interesting for political analysis. Since many scarce goods such as commodity imports,

[1] "Fifteen Years of Economic Policy in Brazil," *Economic Bulletin for Latin America,* IX (November 1964), pp. 196–197.

foreign and domestic credits, as well as long-term investment resources were distributed by government action rather than the market mechanism, the record of actual decisions is a revealing indicator of who had the power to obtain the resources for which various groups competed. In particular, many of these resources were contested between the private sector industrialists and the public-sector economic corporations. Perhaps the major feature of allocation decisions in Brazil during this period was the extent to which the government was able to dominate in this conflict, determining the allocation of resources as it thought best, with very little consideration for vested interests in the private sector. Finally, we will consider the factors conditioning allocations *within* the public sector.

Allocation of Domestic Resources

During the postwar period, the share of the Brazilian public sector in GNP rose very sharply and reached levels which are relatively high for a less-developed country. The federal government's expenditure rose with an income-elasticity of 1.5 percent between 1947 and 1960.[2] That is, for every 1 percent that Brazilian national income grew in this period, the federal government's expenditure grew 1.5 percent. The expenditure of the public sector as a whole rose even more sharply. The consumption and investment of the federal, state, and local governments and of the public economic corporations rose from approximately 16 percent of GNP in 1947–1949 to 27 percent in 1958–1960, an increase of 75 percent.[3] Furthermore, lest it be thought that this expansion was achieved only by budget deficits, because the government lacked the political power to raise taxes or an administrative mechanism to collect them, we should note that the share of government *taxation* in GNP also increased sharply, approximately 50 percent between 1947–1949 and

[2] Antônio Delfim Netto et al, *A Inflação Brasileira e Suas Perspectivas para 1965*, (São Paulo: ANPES, 1965), pp. 79–80.
[3] These and most of the other figures cited in this chapter are from the semi-official Fundação Getúlio Vargas. These are the standard statistics which provide the source for other studies and comparative data collections, for example, by the United Nations. Annual figures on the share of public-sector expenditure in Brazilian GNP are presented in Table 23 of the Statistical Appendix.

1958–1960.[4] As a result of this development, public-sector taxation was approximately 23 percent of GNP by the late 1950's. This is very high in relation to the level of Brazilian per capita income or the size of the foreign-trade sector, two variables which cross section analysis has shown to be highly correlated with the public sector's revenue share in less-developed countries.[5] The Brazilian coefficient of 23 percent compares with a figure of 15 percent suggested by the level of the country's per capita income [6] and a figure of 9 percent indicated by the size of the foreign-trade sector.[7]

As a result of the rapid growth both of the public-sector share and Brazilian GNP, public-sector taxation and expenditures rose in real terms at annual cumulative rates of 9.7 percent and 11.5 percent, respectively, during the period 1947–1960.[8]

In the area of credit allocations, the public sector also demonstrated its ability to appropriate a rising and relatively large share. The banking system's loans were, of course, dominated by the government-controlled *Banco do Brasil.* Table 6 (page 38) presents data on the distribution of bank credit between the private and the public sector. Between the initial and terminal three-year periods, the share of the government and of the public economic corporations in total credits rose almost 65 percent.

The public sector showed an even more dramatic increase in its share of all resources allocated to fixed capital formation. As the public sector increased its share in GNP, the proportion of its expenditure that went to fixed capital formation showed a tendency to rise.[9] The data in Table 7 indicate that the public

[4] *Ibid.* Annual data are presented in Table 24 of the Statistical Appendix.
[5] On per capita income as a determinant of the public-sector revenue share, see Harry Oshima, "The Share of Government in Gross National Product for Various Countries," *American Economic Review* (June 1957); and Karl Deutsch, "Social Mobilization and Political Development," *American Political Science Review* (September 1961). A study by H. H. Hinrichs, "Determinants of Government Revenue Shares in Less-Developed Countries," *Economic Journal* (September 1965), indicates that particularly for countries with per capita income below $300, as in Brazil, the size of the foreign-trade sector provides a statistically better predictor of the government revenue share.
[6] Deutsch, *op. cit.,* p. 498.
[7] Hinrichs, *op. cit.,* pp. 551, 554.
[8] Computed from Tables 23 and 24 in the Statistical Appendix and from data on Brazilian GNP.
[9] Annual data on fixed investment as a proportion of all public-sector ex-

TABLE 6. *The Public Sector's Share in All Credits Granted by the Brazilian Banking System, 1951–1962*

Year	Percent	Three-Year Moving Average
1951	24.6	—
1952	21.2	23.7
1953	25.2	24.2
1954	26.1	26.1
1955	27.1	27.8
1956	30.3	30.4
1957	33.9	32.6
1958	33.6	34.0
1959	34.5	34.6
1960	35.7	37.3
1961	41.6	38.9
1962	39.4	—

Source. Computed from data supplied by the Research Division of SUMOC; 1951 was the initial year in the SUMOC series.

sector took approximately 23 percent of all Brazilian long-term investment in 1947–1949. This percentage rose to 52 percent more than half of the total, in 1958–1960.[10] This sharp increase meant that the vast expansion of public-sector investment activities, discussed below, was possible only by a squeeze, in percentage terms, of the private sector; for the share of aggregate investment in Brazilian GNP did not rise during the postwar period.

Data on capital formation by the major individual investors within the public sector are available for the years 1957–1963. During this period the greater part of capital expenditure went into road construction, the government petroleum company (Petrobrás), the National Development Bank, and construction

penditure are presented in Table 25 of the Statistical Appendix. The federal government's investment expenditure rose with an income-elasticity of 1.7, as compared with a figure of 1.4 for consumption. These data are from *A Inflação Brasileira, loc. cit.*

[10] Another study, EPEA, *O Mercado Brasileiro de Capitais,* (Rio de Janeiro, 1965), pp. 39–40, has also stressed the significant increase and the high level of the percentage of aggregate investment resources commanded by the government.

TABLE 7. *The Public Sector's Share of Aggregate Fixed Capital Formation in Brazil, 1947–1960*

Year	Percent	Three-Year Moving Average
1947	15.8	—
1948	23.3	22.8
1949	29.4	29.3
1950	35.1	29.8
1951	25.0	29.0
1952	26.8	27.0
1953	29.4	26.8
1954	24.3	25.9
1955	24.0	25.4
1956	27.9	32.5
1957	45.6	41.6
1958	51.2	47.8
1959	46.5	52.2
1960	58.8	—

Source. Calculated from data published in *Revista Brasileira de Economia* (March 1962). As stated there, however (pp. 29–31), those figures do not include in the public-sector's expenditures the large amounts involved in construction of Brasília. I have included these figures, available in "Gastos Públicos em Brasília," *Conjuntura Econômica* (December 1962).

of the new capital city of Brasília. Table 8 shows the relative importance accorded each of these activities.

Finally, to complete our picture of the public sector's investment allocations, Table 9 shows the sectoral distribution of the National Development Bank's investments in the years 1952–1962. "Sectors complementing agriculture" refers to some agricultural storage projects, and the relatively small allocation reflects the low priority given to agriculture during this period. "Transportation" consisted mainly of the re-equipping of the Brazilian railroads, which had been purchased from foreign investors. "Basic industries" is largely steel production.[11] In fact, once the railways had been provided with new equipment in the early and middle 1950's, the great bulk of the Development Bank's

[11] Banco Nacional de Desenvolvimento Econômico, *XII Exposição sobre O Programa de Reaparelhamento Econômico* (Rio de Janeiro, 1964), p. 38.

TABLE 8. *Relative Importance of Major Public Sector Fixed Investments, 1957–1963 (Percentage of Total Allocation to These Four Areas)*

Year	Roads	Petrobrás	National Development Bank	Brasília
1957	35%	17%	35%	13%
1958	32	24	26	18
1959	31	22	24	23
1960	25	29	15	31
1961	37	40	12	11
1962	43	21	13	24
1963	44	32	24	—

Sources. Data on Brasília were available from "Gastos Públicos em Brasília"; data on road construction were supplied by Fundação Getúlio Vargas; data on Petrobrás were kindly supplied by that organization's Economics Department; data on the National Development Bank are from the *XII Exposição sôbre o Programa de Reaparelhamento Econômico* (Rio de Janeiro, 1964), hereafter cited as *XII Exposição.*

TABLE 9. *Sectoral Distribution of Investments by the Brazilian National Development Bank, 1952–1962*

Sector	Percent
"Sectors complementing agriculture"	2
Transportation	29
"Basic industries"	37
Electricity	32

Source. XII Exposição, p. 31.

resources went to four public-sector projects—two in steel and two in electricity. Before discussing the factors behind these decisions, however, let us consider the allocation of imported resources.

Allocation of Imported Resources

In screening commodity imports, government policy was based on the criteria of reducing consumer goods imports and giving priority to raw materials and equipment. Consumer goods imports, it was felt, were often only luxury or semiluxury products. Curtailing imports of raw materials and equipment, however, would lower production in the economy. It was also believed that domestic supply was much more price-elastic for consumer goods than for many intermediate and capital goods. Hence import substitution in these products could proceed more rapidly and with less upward pressure on prices. For these reasons consumer goods were accorded a low priority in the allocation of foreign exchange. Table 10 shows the effects of this

TABLE 10. *Commodity Distribution of Brazilian Imports*

Commodity Group	Percentage			
	1938–1939	*1948–1950*	*1954–1956*	*1957–1959*
Food, beverages, tobacco	15	18	16	13
Final consumer products	11	9	3	3
Fuels	13	13	21	21
Other raw materials	30	24	30	31
Equipment	30	35	30	32
Others	1	1	—	—
	100	100	100	100

Source. Computed from data in Hélio Schlittler Silva, "Comércio Exterior do Brasil e Desenvolvimento Econômico," *Revista Brasileira de Ciências Sociais* (March 1962), Table 7. Choice of periods in the table is dictated by the arrangement in this source.

policy in changing the composition of Brazilian commodity imports during these years.

Government allocation preferences are also revealed in the choice of products which were accorded favorable exchange-rate treatment under the system established in 1953. Five categories received the bulk of the most preferential (*câmbio de custo*) rate: wheat, petroleum, newsprint, equipment, and debt service for foreign-financed capital goods imports. Table 11 shows the pattern of allocations.

Wheat and petroleum were accorded preferential import treatment because the government believed that the general price level was especially sensitive to their price movements. Hence their inclusion in the list of favored imports reflects an anti-inflationary effort. Newsprint was included because of the

TABLE 11. *Allocation of the Preferential Exchange Rate,*
1955–1960

	Percentage				
Year	Equipment and Financial Charges	Petroleum	Wheat	Newsprint	Others
1955	46	27	20	6	1
1956	50	32	13	4	1
1957	54	28	11	5	2
1958	52	28	12	4	2
1959	57	24	14	3	2
1960	57	23	13	3	4

Source. Computed from data supplied by the Research Division of SUMOC.

government's desire, for reasons discussed in Chapter 8, to cater to the newspapers. A notable feature of Table 11, however, is the large allocations—more than half the total—for equipment, both for current purchases and for debt service of past imports. This decision reflected the government's effort to promote capital formation by lowering the cost of investment goods.

The government also determined allocation of the substantial foreign commercial credits Brazil received in the postwar period. In 1953 the decision was made to reserve such credits for capital formation, and to exercise direct controls in channeling these credits to sectors deemed of highest economic priority.[12] This allocation of foreign loans was important for the amounts involved both directly and also indirectly, because of the strategic place of such loans in many Brazilian investment projects. By controlling the allocation of foreign-financed equipment, the government also influenced allocation of complementary investments in construction, domestically produced equipment, and "cash and carry" equipment imports.

Between 1955 and 1961, for which data are available, Brazil received a total of 2180 million dollars in foreign commercial credits. Less than 5 percent of this finance went to areas outside

[12] The Monetary Authority declared that only loans which it approved could be assured of foreign exchange for debt service, and as a result foreign lenders would extend credits only for projects sanctioned by the government.

of the government's priorities.[13] Table 12 shows the sectoral pattern of allocations. As in the case of the Development Bank's allocations, presented in Table 9, electricity, steel, and transportation received most of these foreign credits.

TABLE 12. *Allocation of Foreign Equipment Credits, 1955–1961*

Sector	Percentage
Electricity	16
Steel	16
Automotive industry	23
Railways and airlines	10
Petroleum [a]	3
Heavy equipment industries	1
Others (mostly chemical and metallurgical industries)	31

Source. "Fifteen Years of Economic Policy in Brazil," *Economic Bulletin for Latin America,* IX (November 1964), pp. 174–175.

[a] The relatively small amount of foreign finance allocated to petroleum does not imply a low government priority but rather reflected the reluctance of foreign lenders to finance the growth of the Brazilian government oil company, which had emerged in atmosphere of conflict with the international oil firms. Lack of foreign credits hardly deterred the *Petrobrás'* expansion, however, for the government simply gave it highest priority to pay with cash for its equipment imports.

The Pattern of Allocation Decisions

There are several striking features to the government allocational decisions just described.[14] First, the public sector was able

[13] Calculated from "Fifteen Years of Economic Policy in Brazil," pp. 174–175.

[14] Any ex post analysis of policy runs the danger of discerning a purposeful pattern in what were really a series of *ad hoc* individual decisions. A particularly misleading picture may arise because intellectuals attached to the political elite may be charged with the task of developing a rationale and ascribing broad purposes to policy decisions which "just happened," or which happened for reasons very different from the official or intellectuals' version. Something akin to this does seem to have occurred in the case of the Brazilian inflation. Chapter 10 discusses this in terms of structural features of Brazilian politics which led the policy-making process to undertake a level of commitments which exceeded available real resources; but some Brazilian intellectuals have interpreted the inflation as a

to appropriate a large share of GNP and an even higher percentage in credit and long-term investment resources. Other examples of the public sector's ability to safeguard its own interests are provided in the large allocations of foreign equipment credits and of Development Bank resources to electricity, steel, and railways. These "sectors" are actually government corporations. If we recalculate the data of Table 12 to see how much of the foreign equipment credits went to these corporations and how much went to private-sector industrialists, we find that the government corporations received approximately 62 percent of the total.[15]

Most of the equipment imports at the preferential exchange-rate also went to public-sector corporations rather than to private industrialists. The government corporations established in such areas as petroleum, steel, railways, and electricity were given automatic rights to privileged equipment importation. Thus these industries, all heavy users of equipment, went to the head of the queue—it was only after their requests had been satisfied that private industrialists could present their petitions. In fact, a 1961 survey of 137 large private-sector Brazilian companies disclosed that only 25 percent had received preferential exchange-rate treatment for their equipment imports.[16] The fact that special policy support for industrialization went largely to *public* corporations rather than private industrialists has been

purposeful effort to generate forced savings. Still, even if individual issues were dealt with in an *ad hoc* fashion and some policy decisions "just happened," this does not preclude the existence of a pattern which reflects the underlying political and other conditions that in fact constrain these decisions. In the extreme case, even if policy-makers deal with successive problems in a purely random manner, these external conditions will dictate a nonrandom pattern to their decisions, as they encounter the political constraints which indicate what is feasible and what is not. In the present case of Brazilian allocation decisions, as we will see below, the policy-makers did indeed have a reasonably clear picture of their goals, while political conditions (which are particularly instructive for analysis of Brazilian politics) permitted the emergence of a consistent policy.

[15] This figure was arrived at from the data in Table 12 and from material in the original source, "Fifteen Years of Economic Policy in Brazil," *loc. cit.*, from which the equipment imports for highway construction, maritime shipping, alkalis, and ore export equipment, all public-sector corporations, were included.

[16] Raimar Richers et al., *O Impacto da Ação do Govêrno sôbre as Emprêsas Brasileiras* (Rio de Janeiro, 1963), pp. 82, 17, 26.

overlooked, however, by many observers, who have spoken indiscriminately of policy favoring the "industrial sector," and interpreted this as evidence of the *private* industrialists' strong political position.[17]

Another aspect of government allocation decisions is the effort to promote economically productive activities and development. Import policy favored products such as raw materials and equipment, which were considered essential for production and capital formation. This was done by various devices: quantitative regulation of imports, preferential exchange-rate arrangements, and reserving the country's debt-servicing capacity for equipment loans. The government also demonstrated this interest in investment by allocating an increasing percentage of its own resources for capital formation.

Finally, some consistent features also run through the government choices in allocating these investment resources. Investment was overwhelmingly directed to infrastructure activities in electricity and transportation. At the same time, the concept of infrastructure was broad, encompassing "basic industries" in such fields as steel and petroleum and to a lesser extent, chemicals and metallurgical industries. Finally, we noted the very large expenditures for construction of Brasília. These allocation decisions were determined largely by two sets of considerations: an effort to establish or expand domestic productive capacity in several industries believed essential for development, and a desire to exclude foreign investors from control of certain sectors of the national economy.

"Bottlenecks" and "Basic Industries"

As noted earlier, the effort to maintain supply of many products above the levels permitted by available foreign exchange impelled the government toward a policy of import substitution. This involved direct support for certain industries (e.g., automobiles) to produce a commodity whose imports were absorbing large amounts of foreign currency, and it entailed general measures to help the economy expand output and initiate pro-

[17] See, for example, Luciano Martins, "Aspectos Políticos da Revolução Brasileira," *Revista Civilisação Brasileira*, 2, pp. 27–28.

duction of many new products previously supplied by importation.

In making its allocation decisions, the government had available several economic studies prepared in the 1940's and early 1950's. These were the reports of economic and engineering groups—the Abbink Mission, the Joint Brazilian-American Commission, and the ECLA-National Development Bank Joint Study. Other studies of specific industries were carried out by working groups in the National Industrial Development Council, and by various *ad hoc* groups appointed in the President's Office and in the National Development Bank. These studies were to be of decisive importance in orienting government allocations during the 1950's.

Although they sometimes differed in their individual orientations, these study groups came to the same general conclusions: without large investments in infrastructure, the Brazilian economy would soon encounter bottleneck conditions constraining its expansion. The sectors most commonly cited were electricity and transportation (rail, road, and shipping). The study groups in the President's Office and the National Development Bank, which were staffed by Brazilians and reflected a domestic approach to the country's economic problems, postulated another set of potential bottlenecks and high priorities. This was a list of basic industries to produce industrial raw materials such as steel, petroleum, chemicals, and nonferrous metals.

This basic-industries approach was part of a pervasive ideology of economic development and modernization which influenced government allocations from the late 1940's and reached its culmination in the "Target Plan" (Progama de Metas) whose projects were formulated in the early 1950's and implemented in 1957–1961 under President Kubitschek. The focus on modernization is seen in several ways. First, the ideology emphasized the need for Brazilian industrialization, for it felt that industrial development was the hallmark of a modern economy. Neglect of agriculture was a prominent unstated attitude of this approach to Brazil's economic future. Introduction of modern industrial technology was stressed not only for its higher productivity but also as a demonstration that Brazilians were capable of mastering the technological complexities of the modern world. On both grounds, industries such as steel and petroleum fit into this picture. They were considered to be the essence of modern "complex technology"; and the ideology assumed that the development of domestic supply of industrial raw materials would be a strategic step toward general industrial progress.

To these ideological convictions orienting the economic administrators toward the basic industries was added another consideration. The balance-of-payments problem was very much prominent in the mind of these civil servants. Following their experience in the 1930's and World War II, when Brazil had not been able to attain desired levels of imports, they feared that foreign-exchange shortage and limited raw-materials supply might constrain the economy's expansion. A straightforward nationalistic orientation was also present. Import substitution of industrial raw materials was desired in order to reduce, if not end, Brazilian dependence on foreign trade conditions and foreign lenders. This motive received strong support as the result of an experience in the early 1950's. The Brazilian government had agreed to the studies of the Joint Brazilian-American Commission because it believed it had received a commitment from the United States for project loans to implement the Commission's recommendations. When the Eisenhower Administration took office, however, these loans were not forthcoming, either from the American government or from the international agencies. As a result, the Brazilian government found itself unable to carry out the program. This frustrating experience and the chronic balance-of-payments crisis forced the economic administrators to consider the contingency that insufficient export receipts might prevent the economy from receiving needed raw materials. In such a case, the level of output in the economy would be directly dependent on the availability of foreign credits.

These themes are exemplified in the large government allocations to two "basic industries," steel and automobiles. With the automotive industry, both aims—import substitution and the avoidance of constraints on growth elsewhere in the economy —were present. In the early 1950's, when the project was first discussed, vehicles constituted one of the largest commodity groups on the import list. Furthermore, the original plans for the automotive industry conceived of it largely in terms of trucks and reflected an effort to overcome a potential transportation bottleneck. Finally, the automotive industry had a special ideological appeal, for to Brazilian opinion it represented par excellence the industry characteristic of a "modern" economy.

In the case of steel, similar motivations were present. The initial support for steel came from the Brazilian military in the 1930's, in the interest of national security and in the belief that domestic steel supply would be a strong stimulus to industrialization and general economic modernization.[18] The idea was soon incorporated in Brazilian nationalist ideology that steel is the most basic of all basic industries, since physical shortages of steel or sharply rising import costs would inhibit the entire industrialization effort. Hence both the Brazilian military and the economic administrators in the Development Bank stressed the importance of domestic steel capacity for national development.

Nationalist Ideology and the Exclusion of Foreign Capital

Another key factor influencing government allocation decisions was the desire to reduce the role of foreign capital in certain "strategic" economic sectors. A clear case occurred with the large government investments in railways. These were purchased in the early postwar years from the foreign companies which had previously dominated this sector. There has been some subsequent ambivalence about these nationalizations; elite opinion has never decided whether the government expelled the foreigners or whether the foreigners once more exploited the Brazilians by receiving an outrageous price for their "scrap iron." At the time, however, these purchases were hailed as ending foreign domination in a "strategic sector."

Electricity is another example. As indicated in Table 9, approximately one-third of the Development Bank's loans went for electricity projects. These large investments were necessary, however, only because the government denied the foreign-owned electricity companies rates adequate to keep pace with

[18] We should note two important characteristics which make a domestic steel industry more appropriate in Brazil than in some other less-developed countries. Brazil has large reserves of high-quality iron ore; and the Brazilian market has been large enough to permit integrated production at optimal scale.

the inflation. With the ensuing low profit levels and atmosphere of political insecurity, the foreign electricity companies did not expand capacity sufficiently for growing demand.[19] As a result, public-sector corporations entered this sector, which took a large fraction of the Development Bank's total resources.

A similar motivation lay behind the large public-sector investments in petroleum, which claimed approximately 25 percent of the major public-sector fixed investments listed in Table 10. The *Petrobrás* investments were so large that they sometimes exceeded the *entire* annual investment program of the National Development Bank. In the early 1950's the government confronted the very large foreign-exchange allocations for petroleum imports and the prospect that future balance-of-payments crises might cause fuel shortages that would restrict activity in the entire economy. Import substitution was decided upon, particularly for petroleum refining. An extremely vigorous debate in public opinion and a nationalist stand by the military, however, determined that the government should establish a public corporation rather than permit the international oil companies to control the petroleum industry. Again, hostility to foreign capital determined a major decision of allocation policy.

Finally, the large governmental allocations for construction of Brasília were dictated neither by an effort at breaking bottlenecks to growth nor by antipathy toward foreign capital. This enormous project, which claimed a large share of all public-sector investment and as much as 10 percent of *total* Brazilian capital formation during the years of its construction,[20] was decided mainly because of the President's strong personal enthusiasm and the favorable reaction which it aroused for a time in

---

[19] Cf. Judith Tendler's summary of the reasons for the failure of the major foreign electricity company to expand its generating capacity [*The Rise of Public Power in Brazil*, (Ph.D. dissertation, Columbia University, 1966), p. 3.]. "The company's principal problem was the impossibility of securing protection against inflation for the price of its product. The intractibility of the rate problem and the consequent insufficiency of supply was in considerable proportion a result of the foreign ownership of the company." Although the government made certain accommodations to the company—notably special rate surcharges and preferential exchange-rate allocations—to enable it to continue operation, political uncertainties inhibited the company from expanding its generating capacity (*ibid.*, pp. 64–65, p. 79).

[20] Computed from data in "Gastos Públicos em Brasília."

public opinion. Support from organized political groups or parties for this large allocation was almost entirely absent.[21] This case clearly has important implications concerning the power of the Presidency in Brazilian politics, but before we discuss this, let us consider the political structure within which these allocation decisions were reached.

The Political Context of Allocation Decisions

By this time, the pattern may appear clear-cut, but no grand design should be imputed. Almost without exception, taxes were raised and resources were allocated within the context of specific sectoral problems. The sequence of events generally went as follows. First, problem areas which appeared to require policy action were identified and discussed within the higher civil service and the Presidential entourage. The choice of problems was usually suggested either by government's pressing administrative needs (e.g., regulating the foreign-exchange market); by currents in elite opinion (e.g., the *Petrobrás*); or, in the case of Brasília, from within the Presidency. Interest groups played almost no role in the selection of problem areas for policymaking.[22]

These specific problems were then studied by economists and engineering experts (*técnicos*) in the Development Bank, the Monetary Authority, the Finance Ministry, or the President's Office. Next, or sometimes concomitantly with the technical study phase, the issues were taken up for wider consideration in the newspapers and other channels of the political communications process. In the ensuing discussion, decisions were reached, guided by preferences within the Presidency and influential

---

[21] For a similar interpretation of the importance of President Kubitschek's personal commitment in providing the pressure for Brasília, see Albert O. Hirschman, *Journeys Toward Progress: Studies of Economic Policy-Making in Latin America* (New York, 1963), p. 83. Regional interests expecting to benefit from transfer of the country's political and administrative capital supported the project, but it was strongly opposed by representatives of the states expecting to lose, particularly Rio de Janeiro. Consequently, in terms of balance of support, there was probably a stalemate, and the President, who had provided the first serious impetus for the project to begin with, was the determining factor.

[22] Cf. a similar comment by Hirschman, pp. 234–235.

opinion's interpretations of the "objective" needs of the situation and the means available for dealing with it.[23]

As suggested by our discussion of the ideologically chosen "basic industries" and the antipathy toward foreign capital in "strategic sectors," official preferences and the interpretations of the country's "needs" were very much influenced by a nationalist ideology which has dominated Brazilian politics. Consensus on economic ideology served to orient decision-makers in their choice of policy problems and solutions, and also, by legitimating policy decisions, the consensus limited political conflict in their acceptance. The major exception here was the *Petrobrás*, whose establishment aroused intensive discussion among the politicians, administrators, and military and within the newspapers and broader public opinion. This case, however, served as a rallying point for the modernizing intelligentsia and political elite. Once the issue was decided on nationalist lines, it proved a milestone in the development of this ideology's dominant position in elite opinion.

The vastly expanded economic role of the public sector was achieved relatively easily within this context. In effect, a few major decisions were taken: that economic growth required an improved road system; that foreign companies should not dominate the petroleum industry; that domestic steel production was a *sine qua non* for economic development. Once made, these decisions had macroeconomic implications reaching farther than was realized. Since these projects were usually capital-intensive and of large minimum scale, the public sector's investment commitments had to rise sharply. Similarly, because the government was the only domestic institution able to mobilize sufficient resources to expel foreign capital from sectors such as railroads or petroleum, the decisions on Brazilian ownership had the direct im-

[23] In his discussion of the Brazilian policy-making process, Hirschman, pp. 72–86, gives an excellent account of such a campaign, in connection with the establishment of the SUDENE, the Development Agency for the backward Northeast Region. Almost all the standard features are present: the "technical report" by an economic administrator, the battles waged in the principal Rio and São Paulo newspapers (pp. 81, 88), the sorting out of political support within the context of public opinion rather than of interest-group alliances (p. 81). Finally, the President went along with elite opinion, although this meant turning against former political allies among the state governors in the Northeast region (p. 86).

plication of a much larger economic role for the government. Because the share of aggregate investment in GNP did not rise, these decisions led to a greater percentage for the public sector in capital formation.

The main features of this allocation pattern were established by the early 1950's. It was given special impetus after 1956 by President Kubitschek, who had a strong personal leaning toward these policy goals. Although this President certainly helped direct allocation decisions along the lines we have described, too much stress should not be laid on his presence, to the neglect of the other features discussed. *All* major economic policy decisions of the post-1947 period—import controls on criteria of productive "essentiality"; establishment of the major government corporations (the Development Bank, the *Petrobrás*, and the transportation sector agencies) with earmarked sources of revenue and investment autonomy; and the plans for the automotive industry—had been taken by the end of 1954, under the second Getúlio Vargas administration.

POLITICAL CONSTRAINTS ON ALLOCATION POLICY

In most of these allocation decisions, the government had adequate support from the politicians in the Congress. They were usually carried along by the newspaper campaigns surrounding key allocation decisions and were convinced of the practical necessity and the ideological value of the measures. In cases where some politicians did oppose administration measures, the President usually had ample carrot-and-stick inducements to win support.

In this political context, private-sector industrialists were not able to stand in the way of the large expansion in the scope of the government's controls and regulation, or to curb its direct investment and production activities. Apart from its control over the "commanding heights" of the economy, the Brazilian public sector came to carry on important activities which even in many "mixed economies" remain the preserve of the private sector.

The industrialists were also unable to exert much influence in the way the government allocated the resources it brought under its control. Indeed, as noted, a large proportion of these was appropriated by the public sector itself. The pattern was set soon after World War II. The Confederation of Industries' proposals for postwar economic policy had called upon the government to give priority to the existing industries in future development. Their claims were simply turned aside, however; and throughout the period, private-sector petitions were placed at the bottom of the list, to be considered only after the government's priorities had been satisfied. The operation of the National Development Bank is another example. The Finance Minister who played an important role in formulating the original plans for the Bank was a prominent private-sector industrialist. The Development Bank was conceived of as a major supplier of long-term finance to private industry, and the Bank was financed largely by a special income tax paid mainly by corporations. Some loans were made to the private sector, but these amounted to relatively little in terms of the Bank's total resources. Between 1952 and 1964, approximately 84 percent of the Development Bank's finance went to public-sector projects.[24] In instances where private firms did benefit from government allocation policy, these were "basic industries" within the private sector —metallurgy, cement, chemicals—which fit in with the government's own preferences. The older, well-established industries such as textiles and food processing, which might have been expected to constitute "vested interests," received almost nothing.

The only special groups to which government allocation policy did cater were the newspapers and the military. As noted earlier, newsprint was accorded preferential import conditions, and the military also had a position of special influence. Their attitude was important in deciding the large allocations for steel and petroleum, and the military ministries' budget increased proportionately with GNP throughout this period.[25] Apart from

[24] This was computed from data in constant cruzeiros on the Bank's investment activities in the period 1952–1964. These figures are available in Banco Nacional de Desenvolvimento Econômico, *XIII Exposição sôbre O Programa de Reaparelhamento Econômico* (Rio de Janeiro, 1965), p. 17.
[25] Data on the military budget appear in successive issues of the *Anuário Estatístico*. If we consider the *level* of military expenditure, we find that it constituted an average of 23 percent of all federal expenditures in the period 1956–1960. (Data are from *A Inflação Brasileira*, pp. 106–107.) This compared with a figure of 26 percent of federal expenditure allotted to fixed capital formation. Had it not been for circumstances which made for a relatively secure external situation, the share of military expenditure

these cases, which are discussed in Chapter 7, what is perhaps most remarkable about Brazilian allocation decisions is the government's freedom from interest-group pressures. Indeed, most of the government's allocations went for totally *new* industries which had no political existence or support outside of the government and elite opinion. For example, very large allocations were made for industries that were initially only a slogan in public opinion (e.g., petroleum) or a worry in the mind of the government *técnicos* (e.g., automobiles).

It may be argued that since private industrialists benefited indirectly from many government policies, there was "really" an identity of interests. The profits of individual businessmen, however, depended largely on their ability to expand their own capacity in order to supply the booming internal market; and the industrialists would have preferred the more direct support of themselves receiving government loans, foreign credits, and scarce imports. The case of Brasília is perhaps the clearest example of the government deciding allocations as it saw best. Whereas the industrialists might see or be convinced of the need for government steel-making or road construction, they did not appreciate the need for Brasília. Nevertheless, with the strong personal support of the President, the project was carried.

Another example of the government's ability to take its own view of the country's needs and resist particular pressures that might interfere with its realization occurred with the capital goods industry. Despite the domestic industry's opposition, throughout most of the postwar period the government permitted importation of foreign equipment without tariffs and, indeed, under preferential exchange rates.[26] Furthermore, al-

could have been much higher. In his study of the economic development of Bulgaria in the very different security situation of the pre-1914 Balkans, for example, Alexander Gerschenkron concludes that "there is little doubt that concentration on foreign and military policy effectively obstructed serious preoccupation with the industrial development of the country." In contrast with Brazil, where almost all of foreign capital inflow went for capital formation, in Bulgaria the figure was approximately 45 percent. See his *Economic Backwardness in Historical Perspective* (Cambridge, Mass., 1962), pp. 229–230.

[26] Contrary to some beliefs, the Brazilian capital goods industry developed relatively early, supplying approximately 60 percent of total equipment demand by the late 1940's. This and the practice of importing foreign

though supplier credits were one of the imports' chief competitive advantages, the government-controlled Development Bank and the *Banco do Brasil* provided almost no finance to help domestic industry compete on this key point.[27]

The government, however, conceived its task primarily to effect major structural changes toward modernizing the economy through creation of new industries such as steel and petroleum. With this emphasis, it had no desire to spend its limited resources in financing the growth of the older and more traditional industries. Hence these industries had to fend for themselves, while the Development Bank looked out for what it considered the best interests of the economy as a whole. Indeed, in promoting growth of its high-priority industries the Bank itself drew heavily upon foreign-financed equipment imports, against the special interests of the domestic equipment industry.

The capital goods industry's reaction to this policy is instructive. The "traditional" political approach of applying pressure on the Executive through the intermediary of favorable Congressmen proved ineffectual. Consequently, the trade association mounted an extensive public relations effort, with inspired press campaigns and contact between trade association staff and government administrators, to convince elite opinion of the close connection between the industry's interests and those of national economic development. Since the industry was in direct rivalry with other basic industries, which were considered to possess equally good if not better development credentials, the appeals were to no avail. As a result, the domestic capital goods industry had to sit by and contend with the competition of favored imports until in the early 1960's, balance-of-payments pressures led the government on its own to restrict foreign-financed equipment imports.

This case also illustrates the integrating effects of nationalist economic ideology and the tactical disadvantage of industrialists

equipment duty-free and under preferential exchange rates are discussed in my study *The Brazilian Capital Goods Industry* (Cambridge, Mass., 1968), Chapters 2, 5, and 6. Some tariffs on equipment imports were instituted after 1957, but these were generally nullified by other legislation and administrative decisions.

[27] As late as 1963, the Development Bank explicitly reaffirmed this policy. See *XII Exposição*, pp. 39–40.

opposing government policies. The equipment industry's campaign against duty-free and special-rate equipment importation appears relatively half-hearted if we compare it with the probable political response of, for example, an American industry seeing the government give preferential terms to foreign competitors. When asked why they have not been more aggressive, Brazilian industry spokesmen generally answer that their country certainly also needs the development of the other sectors on which the government has placed higher priorities. That is, these industrialists, too, subscribe to the prevailing ideology which preaches the necessity for the "basic industries" in Brazilian development. Consequently, they did not argue "capital goods against steel" but only pleaded for "capital goods *and* steel." Hence, when the issue *was* posed in conflicting rather than complementary terms, they were at a serious tactical disadvantage. When the steel industry could expand only on the basis of imported equipment, because foreign suppliers offered credits which Brazilian firms could not match, the domestic industry felt it had to accede to a policy promoting the good of the country as a whole.

Finally, the government exercised this conclusive influence on allocation decisions even though interest-group participation in the decision-making process was often formally institutionalized. To facilitate planning the development of key sectors such as automobiles, the government set up special "Executive Groups" in which private industrialists participated with government administrators. As in the case of the National Tariff Council, however, testimony of all participants agrees that the government representatives usually carried the day in case of conflict. Even more important, the action of the Executive Groups was closely circumscribed by a background of prior decisions, for example, on the general commitment to import-substituting industrialization and on the specific sectors chosen for development. These basic decisions, which provided the framework within which the Executive Groups worked had already been taken, in great measure independently of the private sector, through the process described earlier. In this context, the Executive Groups functioned as technical study groups, analyzing the new industries' markets and the supply conditions necessary to meet them. Private industrialists participated not as representatives voicing business views and interests, but as individuals, usually engineers, with special technical competence on conditions in domestic industry. This is not to say that "politics"—for example, personal connections with the President—played no role at all in the allocation process. The operation of such factors, however, was limited within the framework the government established according to its own criteria. Once this framework was set, "political" factors may have played a role.[28] In fact, however, there were few allegations of corruption in the allocation of incentives for the new industries.

Conclusions

We can now summarize some features of the process in which government allocation decisions were reached in Brazil during this period.

First, in determining priorities for allocation of the wide range of domestic and imported resources which it came to control, the government was concerned to promote the country's economic development. We saw evidence for this in the preferential allocation of foreign exchange for equipment imports and in the rising share of capital formation in the government's expenditure. The public sector was also politically able to increase substantially its share in national product and especially in investment. And in allocating these resources, the government had substantial political autonomy, and could make large allotments to the projects which were believed most likely to promote

---

[28] For example, having made the basic decision to establish a domestic automotive industry, the government set up an Executive Group to plan its characteristics. Taking into account replacement needs and future income growth, this group estimated the annual market to be supplied. Divided into different vehicle categories, this, in turn, constituted a market for a given number of carburetors of various types. Given the characteristics of carburetor manufacture, this output target would imply a number of producing firms with fabricating equipment able to meet certain technical standards. Companies installing capacity with these specifications would qualify for incentives such as preferential-rate equipment importation or loans from the Development Bank. To the extent that personal influence determined the allocation of these incentives, it was at this last stage—in choosing between various investment projects if more than the required number was submitted.

development, to the neglect of "vested interest" in industry or agriculture. This is not a picture of a government either uninterested in promoting economic development or too hamstrung by political pressures to proceed constructively in that direction.

In the absence of determining political pressures—for example, from interest groups—preferences within the Presidency and the currents of elite opinion seem to have been the major influences on economic policy. Elite opinion, in turn, often followed an ideology which presented a picture of the economy to which Brazil should aspire: industrialized, modernized, and independent. It also delineated the means—government promotion of import-substitution in the basic industries, ouster of foreign capital from "strategic sectors"—necessary for its realization. In subsequent chapters we will discuss the political system which made possible the government's dominant position and its relative insulation from interest-group pressures. Now we turn to a case-study which illustrates some features of elite opinion as a major influence on Brazilian economic policy.

CHAPTER 4

Direct Foreign Investment

Hostility toward foreign investment has a long history in Brazilian politics. As early as the 1920's, in the episode of the Itabira Iron Company, feelings within the political elite were strong enough to bar the granting of mining concessions to a foreign company. Economic xenophobia and fear of imperialism continued under Getúlio Vargas through the 1930's, with legislation regulating foreign mining operations. Hostility to foreign investors was not the exclusive property of any single President or clique, however, and the Dutra regime which succeeded Getúlio also restricted profit remission by foreign companies. Discriminatory controls on capital movements by foreign investors and adverse exchange-rate treatment continued through the early 1950's.[1]

In 1955, however, this orientation was changed, and Brazil welcomed private investors to many economic sectors. Seven years later, in 1962, these policies were reversed, and punitive regulations against foreign investment were introduced. In this chapter we will examine the factors which determined government decisions in these cases.

Instruction 113 and the Encouragement of Foreign Private Investment

In 1955 the Monetary Authority instituted Instruction 113, initiating a new policy toward foreign firms establishing manufacturing operations in Brazil. The Instruction modified the

[1] See Werner Baer, *Industrialization and Economic Development in Brazil* (Homewood, Ill., 1965), p. 50 on the Dutra regime, p. 52 on later exchange-rate policy.

exchange-rate system so that foreign private investors in high-priority sectors were accorded more favorable conditions both in making their investments and in profit remission. Equally important, official attitudes changed to create a new investment climate that made foreign companies feel politically secure in Brazil.[2] The major factor influencing the government in the new policy was the desire to use foreign investment as a means of improving the country's deteriorating balance-of-payments situation. In 1955 world coffee prices dropped 30 percent from the peak levels reached during the Korean War and its aftermath. Moreover, foreign supplier credits could not be expected to add greatly to Brazilian imports, for the heavy medium-term debts contracted during the stockpiling years of 1951 and 1952 were being repaid. Public capital flows in these years were *negative;* and the administration in Washington, insisting that private capital flows should be quite sufficient for Brazil's needs, did not hold out any prospect for expanded foreign aid.

At the same time, demand for imported capital goods and raw materials had reached new heights, as a result of the stimulus to import substitution given by Instruction 70. The Finance Minister and the senior economic administrators feared, however, that investment and growth might be hampered by insufficient capacity to import. In these conditions, long-term investment by foreign manufacturing firms was considered to offer a promising source of additional foreign exchange. Such investment also had two additional advantages commending it to Brazilian policy-makers. First, it was believed that foreign capital would make a net addition to investment resources for import substitution. Second, direct investment would bring with it know-how in the new, "technologically complex" industries which the government wanted to develop.

In these circumstances, the previous policy toward direct foreign investment was changed. The effects were not far from the policy-makers' hopes. As Table 13 indicates, direct foreign private investment increased sharply after 1955, and during the next seven years 714 million dollars of such capital inflow were attracted to Brazil.

2 See Lincoln Gordon and Engelbert Grommers, *United States Manufacturing Investment in Brazil* (Boston, Mass., 1962), for a discussion of the effects of Instruction 113 in attracting direct foreign private investment.

TABLE 13. *Direct Foreign Private Investment in Brazil, 1947–1961*

Year	Millions of Dollars
1947	36
1948	25
1949	5
1950	3
1951	−4
1952	9
1953	22
1954	11
1955	43
1956	90
1957	144
1958	110
1959	124
1960	98
1961	108

Source. Werner Baer, *Industrialization and Economic Development in Brazil* (Homewood, Ill., 1965), p. 107.

The government maintained control of these resources, soliciting foreign capital and according it the favorable terms of the Instruction only for investments in sectors it considered of high priority. As Table 14 indicates, almost 90 percent of this invest-

TABLE 14. *Sectoral Distribution of Foreign Investment under Instruction 113, 1955–1962*

Industry	Percent
Automotive	46
Steel, nonferrous metals, chemicals, cement, mechanical and electrical equipment, pharmaceutical	40
Food products	2
Textile	4
Other	8
	100

Source. Calculated from SUMOC data published in *Relatório do Banco do Brasil* (Rio de Janeiro, 1964), p. 211.

ment was in the automotive and the basic industries. This was the new government policy toward direct foreign investment. How was it able politically to implement such a program?

In the first instance, the original measures taken in this direction were made by a discretionary decree of the Monetary Authority, independent of legislative sanction. At the same time, the measure was generally supported in the higher bureaucracy and the broader political elite. The Finance Minister who was the policy's principal architect, Eugênio Gudin, had great personal prestige as a technical analyst of Brazil's economic problems.[3] Although the younger and more nationalistic economists considered him too "orthodox," this was before the emergence of Celso Furtado to national prominence, and they did not have a spokesman of sufficient stature to challenge Gudin on technical grounds. The Finance Minister's reputation for personal honesty also carried great weight in broader ranges of the political elite. The President at the time was Café Filho, successor to Getúlio, and even outside the President's immediate political circle, elite opinion was going through one of the recurrent periods in which it welcomed a "technical" and morally austere administration, in contrast to the previous one of "politics" and "corruption."

Although the particular conditions present at the policy's initiation soon passed, the policy itself was maintained by the next President, Kubitschek, with elite consensus, through the late 1950's. First, the policy was interpreted as a necessity imposed by the balance-of-payments problem, as export receipts continued to lag through the second half of the decade. For this reason, direct foreign investments were always referred to as imports "*sem cobertura cambial*"—that is, imports not entailing demand for additional foreign exchange—and hence a net addition to import capacity. The policy was also given legitimacy by its contributions to national economic development. The President believed that the goals of his administration's Target Plan for development could not be reached without foreign capital

---

[3] Gudin also had his political side as a vigorous opponent of Getúlio Vargas. This helped make him acceptable to the regime succeeding Vargas. What commended him to the position of Finance Minister, however, was the enormous prestige which his technical competence carried both within and beyond his own political circle.

and know-how. The industries where foreign investment was making itself felt more noticeably—automobiles and heavy equipment—were among those accorded high priority for developing a modern economy, but they were not considered too "strategic" to be left in foreign hands.

The policy constituted a choice between the two priorities of antipathy to foreign capital and national economic development. The value placed on economic development was so great during these years—indeed, even the ECLA-National Development Bank projections of the early 1950's had admitted an extensive role to foreign capital in some sectors—that the priority of economic development dominated. Furthermore, it was felt that by establishing domestic production in these products, albeit in foreign hands, Brazil was taking a decisive step toward liberation from dependence on export demand and foreign credit availability. The desire to establish these industries in Brazil was so great that Development Bank loans and equity participation were authorized for certain foreign firms (for example, in heavy electrical equipment) which the government wanted especially to attract.

These were the considerations which led the President and most of the political elite to support the policy. Testimony of the larger Brazilian private "economic groups," trade associations, and government officials indicates, however, that it was generally opposed by the domestic industrialists. Some data on the resistance to Instruction 113 are presented in Table 15. These figures actually understate the extent of the opposition,

TABLE 15. *Attitudes of Private Brazilian Industrialists to Instruction 113*

Attitude	Percent
Against	38
Mixed feelings	32
In favor	30

Source. A 1961 attitude survey by Raimar Richers et al., published in *Impacto da Ação do Govêrno sôbre as Emprêsas Brasileiras* (Rio de Janeiro, 1963), p. 119, Table 7-B-b.

for the tabulation, by number, obscures the fact that hostility to the measure was greatest among the largest and most powerful Brazilian firms.[4]

The first reaction of the larger domestic industrialists to Instruction 113 and the prospect of wide-scale entry by foreign firms was panic. Foreign companies were believed to possess enormous competitive advantages; and the prospect of having to compete with them within the Brazilian market filled many industrialists with terror. This reaction was particularly marked among the more important domestic manufacturing groups, the elite of Brazilian industry. First, they believed that foreign firms would be more likely to enter their own sectors of large-scale or capital-intensive production. Hence they feared for the monopoly positions which they often held in those industries. More generally, they felt that their position of preeminence within the national manufacturing sector was threatened. As the nationalist ideologists who gave formal expression to these apprehensions put it: there was an "inevitable contradiction of interests" between the "national bourgeoisie" and the "international trusts." In consequence of these fears, Brazilian industrialists soon attempted to prevail upon the government to repeal Instruction 113 and subsequent legislation which confirmed it.

The industrialists threatened with entry by foreign firms began by contacts with the President's Office and executive agencies such as the Monetary Authority to explain their plight. This communication was undertaken both by prominent individual businessmen and by the Confederation of Industries. The industrialists' weak political position is seen in the fact that these contracts were viewed by all participants more as petitions than as pressure, with an "either . . . or" implication and the threat of sanctions. Business groups simply did not control enough votes to adopt anything like an aggressive stance. In this context, the government heard the petitions and sent the industrialists home muttering about the government that had either been

---

[4] This was emphasized in interviews with trade association and government officials. The high percentage of "Mixed feelings" in Table 15 probably reflects the ambivalence caused by the fact that, although 58 percent of respondents indicated in another question (Richers, *op. cit.*, p. 120) that the Instruction had promoted Brazilian economic development, they were opposed to it on other grounds.

"bought" by the foreign capitalists or that "did not understand" their problems.

We should note several aspects of this process. The industrialists' pleas were seen by the government as representing particular interests which should not interfere with a policy promoting the general welfare. The latter was manifest to all in the country's rapid industrial development, in which the automotive industry, which became the symbol of direct foreign investment, was playing a leading role. Only in the few cases when industrialists could make a case involving broader issues than their individual predicament did the government respond to their requests.[5] Indeed, Instruction 113 had led to achievements so highly esteemed because of the high priority accorded to economic development, that business opposition was, in anticipation, relatively muted. Especially the Confederation of Industries, the general spokesman for the industrialists, felt that it could not be associated publicly with an extensive attack on a policy that was achieving goals with such extensive support in public opinion.

In understanding this process, we should note that some arguments *were* available framed in terms of the general welfare which business interests could have used to buttress their position. Some nationalist intellectuals and legislators were voicing the view that foreign private investment would reduce rather than increase national independence. This is, Instruction 113 was permitting international monopoly capital to dominate Brazil from within the country rather than as previously, only from without. Throughout these years, however, these voices remained outside the center of elite opinion.

[5] There were two notable cases when domestic industrialists convinced the government to drop foreign investment projects. One episode involved the opposition of the Matarazzo group to the investment plans of the American Can Company. Here the opposition was unusually able in mobilizing a public opinion campaign, complete with student demonstrations, and successfully portrayed its case as going far beyond its own limited interests. Another incident involved the effort of the Hilton interests to establish a hotel in Brazil. Here the case of the domestic businessmen was greatly strengthened by the fact that hotels did not rank high on Brazilian ideology's list of glamorous and "technically complex" industries. Hence it did not carry a priority high enough to justify lifting the taboo against foreign investment.

The dominant factor here was the orientation of the President, and this case permits us to see him in the key role of leader in the political communications process. As noted, the administration was committed to a development program for which foreign investment was believed necessary. Consequently, the President chose to ignore and isolate themes in elite opinion which might have prejudiced his policy goals. We can appreciate the importance of the President here by considering a contrasting episode when he felt that his program *was* threatened by foreign pressures. This occurred in 1958–1959, when balance-of-payments pressures forced the government to enter negotiations with the International Monetary Fund. Fearing that the fiscal and monetary measures proposed by the Fund would jeopardize his development goals, the President took the lead in mobilizing public opinion in a vigorous campaign against the "foreign pressures attempting to limit Brazilian development." This maneuver "tied his hands" and made acceptance of the stabilization program politically impossible.

Restrictions on Direct Foreign Investment

In 1962 a new profits-remission law was enacted which ended the previous policy of welcoming foreign capital. The process leading to this change is especially interesting, for it shows how the same political structure discussed earlier could well lead to very different policies. In particular, we will see the importance for policy formulation of changes within the Presidency and within elite opinion.

The new policy stemmed from the radicalization of Brazilian politics that began with the election in 1960 of a new President, Jânio Quadros. Several months after taking office, Quadros resigned and was succeeded by the Vice-President, João Goulart, head of the PTB (Partido Trabalhista Brasileira) party. This party has had its orientation in more radical Brazilian nationalist ideology, and several nationalist ideologists became advisors within the Presidential entourage.

The ideology that was thus given preferential political access has taken a special approach toward foreign capital. Giving considerable prominence to the theme of imperialism, nationalist intellectuals have considered foreign capital both central to all Brazilian political and economic issues, and enormously prejudicial to the country's development.

We can gain an idea of the importance attributed to foreign capital from the fact that one prominent thinker of the *Instituto Superior de Estudos Brasileiros* (Higher Institute of Brazilian Studies) has written the history of modern Brazil almost entirely in terms of relations with the International Trusts.[6] Not only is foreign investment accorded a wholly pernicious role, but its importance as a threat to national interests is considered of extraordinary proportions. The following example suggests the quantitative significance imputed to foreign capital, as well as the way in which the question has sometimes been approached. In a widely read book, the same Brazilian intellectual stated that foreign capital remissions in 1958 amounted to 17.7 billion dollars.[7] This figure differs by a factor of 37 from the statistic published by the Brazilian Monetary Authority! It amounted to

[6] Nelson Werneck Sodré, *Formação Histórica do Brasil* (2d ed., São Paulo, 1963), pp. 341 ff. Sodré may appear a somewhat radical nationalist figure, and the very label "nationalist" may imply the connotation of "extreme" or fanatic. Within the Brazilian context, however, views which may appear "extreme" or atypical elsewhere are well within the mainstream of ideas accepted as self-evident. For an example of the extent to which even "moderate" Brazilian nationalists came to consider it axiomatic that foreign capital should not take a prominent place in their country's development, consider the following statement by Hélio Jaguaribe in a discussion of the pros and cons of foreign investment: "The study will concentrate on analyzing the effects of foreign investment in the promotion of the national development of less-advanced countries. . . . What we shall mean by the words "national development" is not any kind of economic growth; it is rather the kind of growth which leads to maximizing the control of the nation over its own means and resources."

With this sort of definition laid down as a first principle even by "moderates," it would be misleading to consider Sodré's views "extreme" in the Brazilian context. The citation is from Hélio Jaguaribe, "A Brazilian View," in Raymond Vernon (ed.), *How Latin America Views the United States Investor* (New York, 1966), p. 68.

[7] Sodré, p. 379. No source is cited for Sodré's figures, but his presentation, as an aggregate built up from seven different subcategories of foreign capital remissions, all of which are presented to the last dollar, gives it a convincing aura of veracity. We should note that the figure cited is in the second edition of this book, unquestioned or at least unrevised from the first edition. Throughout this period, Sodré continued as an eminent intellectual figure at respected academic institutions.

approximately 115 percent of *total* Brazilian GNP for that year, as estimated by ECLA; and more than 12 times the value of Brazilian exports, which presumably provided the channel for transferring these capital remissions.[8] In addition to its enormous quantitative proportions, foreign capital has been considered to have pervasive, harmful effects. Among those often cited are reduction of Brazilian national income through large transfers abroad; depreciating the exchange rate; intensifying inflation; and reducing the rate of economic growth—aside from compromising Brazilian political autonomy.[9] As such views moved to the center of the Presidential entourage, proposals to restrict foreign investment were inevitably brought to the fore.

The Changed Mood of Elite Opinion

At the same time, these attitudes were no longer isolated from the mainstream of elite opinion or from the views of the economic administrators. Direct foreign investment had been welcomed initially because of its contribution to easing the balance-of-payments problem and to national economic development. Beginning in the early 1960's, however, because of a sharp rise in the burden of capital charges on the balance of payments, foreign capital was perceived as a factor *aggravating* the foreign-exchange shortage. Concurrently, the high priority previously given to economic development was also called into question.

This questioning occurred on two counts in an autonomous movement within the political communications process. One current of opinion, focusing on some aspects of the social change associated with rapid economic growth and on alleged corruption that had accompanied public-sector expansion, declared that the moral costs of the previous economic development outweighed its value. Consequently, greater emphasis was placed on eradica-

---

[8] For the figure given by the Monetary Authority, see Table X-6, *Programa de Ação Econômica do Govêrno Revolucionário* (Rio de Janeiro, 1964), which uses data from the Research Division of SUMOC. The ECLA data are in the *Economic Development of Latin America in the Post-War Period* (United Nations, 1964), p. 113.

[9] Cf. the speeches and articles of a prominent spokesman for this attitude, Sérgio Magalhães, in *Práctica da Emancipação Nacional* (Rio de Janeiro, 1964), esp. pp. 116–120.

tion of graft than on economic development. A second current of opinion also disputed the value of economic development "per se" and declared that basic reforms in Brazilian social, political, and economic structure should take priority as national goals.

The new phase started with the inauguration of Jânio Quadros in 1961. He began his administration with attacks against the corrupt forces present during the previous years of rapid economic development and the "sinister" elements impeding realization of his own program. This contrasted sharply with the political style of President Kubitschek, who had stressed the non-antagonistic aspects of development and had tended to gloss over possible conflict. Public opinion, which had been euphoric about the achievements of national economic development and ignorant of "inevitable social antagonisms," now learned that previous achievements had been purchased only at an enormous moral price and that "true" development would require frontal attack upon reactionary domestic and foreign forces. This focus was sharply intensified when Quadros resigned from the Presidency, with the implication that evil forces had prevented him from realizing necessary "structural" reforms.

At the same time, the intelligentsia in the vanguard of elite opinion were also reconsidering the national situation. They too found that the previous *desenvolvimentismo*—putting primary emphasis on economic development—was no longer morally and emotionally sufficient. Despite fifteen years of rapid economic development and unprecedented technical achievements, they saw that the millennium had still not come; that economic growth had brought with it unanticipated costs; and that many old problems remained, in addition to others created by the very process of successful industrialization. We find a statement of these views in a 1961 essay by a leading Brazilian social thinker.

. . . The final fruit of all this is not development. On the contrary, it consists of the creation of new economic, political, and social privileges with only one innovation: the replacement of the old rural aristocracy by an urban plutocracy, more powerful in the manipulation of power, more selfish . . . , more voracious. The *ancien regime* has undergone severe shocks, but social change rarely takes place in a form assuring justice and social welfare. Unhealthy regional economic and cultural disparities arise in the same country . . . ; social institutions are deformed, mainly in public administration and politics, to cater largely to the pressures . . . of the "entrepreneurs" of development. The most inhuman contrasts between poverty and wealth are accepted . . . .

Behind these events operate powerful forces, installed within the domestic as well as the international structure of power. As in the past an alliance between the rural landlord with traders of tropical products was natural, now it is common to have an alliance between the "entrepreneur" of development with the capitalists, whoever they are and whatever they represent . . . . The Latin American peoples are paying an exorbitant price for "progress" and for "development." [10]

As this indicates, the major themes raised in this critique were that despite rapid economic development, the social and political transformation of society were not proceeding in the right direction. Consequently, political discussion began to stress the need for "basic reforms"—in agriculture, in income distribution, and between geographic regions—to better the position of those who "had been excluded from the benefits of industrialization." As the quotation illustrates, the value of cooperation with foreign capital was also questioned. Indeed, for much of the Brazilian intelligentsia, one of the most important of all "basic reforms" lay in foreign policy. Despite the achievements of national development, strong feelings of dependence persisted vis-à-vis the United States. Hence the need for an "independent foreign policy" was stressed both for its intrinsic importance and because it would help resolve most other problems. Quite apart from the strong feelings anyhow felt against foreign capital, it was felt that ending favorable treatment of foreign investors would be an important step toward national self-assertion.[11]

The intelligentsia's reassessment of Brazil's needs was transmitted to broader ranges of elite opinion through the normal communications channels, particularly the newspapers, and

[10] Florestan Fernandes, *A Sociologia Numa Era de Revolução Social* (São Paulo, 1963), pp. 250–251 (my translation).
[11] Ironically, the "structural" reforms generally advocated by Brazilians resembled those proposed by United States spokesmen under the Alliance for Progress. Both Brazilians and Americans, for example, stressed the need for agrarian, educational, and administrative reforms. Since one crucial reform for the Brazilians was greatly reduced political ties between Brazil and the United States, however, there was a serious built-in difficulty to close collaboration with the United States.

through an important new institution established in the 1950's, the ISEB (Instituto Superior de Estudos Brasileiros). Created within the Ministry of Education and staffed with some of Brazil's ablest nationalist thinkers, its objectives were "the study, teaching, and dissemination of the social sciences . . . with the special objective of applying . . . these sciences to the analysis of and critical understanding of Brazilian reality with a view to . . . the stimulation and promotion of national development." [12] The Institute did provide support for nationalist social science analysis, but more important in the present context, it also disseminated its particular interpretation of "Brazilian reality" widely within the political elite through an intensive program of lectures, courses, seminars, and publications.

As a result of the generalized self-questioning and opening of new perspectives, elite opinion in the early 1960's entered a profound ideological crisis. In contrast with earlier years when consensus on basic issues had been broad enough to facilitate effective policy action, a new period now opened with intense discussion of ideological issues and new policy orientations.[13] At the same time as it became more difficult to resolve issues, moreover, the demands placed upon the policy-making process increased. After 1961, inflation accelerated sharply, the import situation deteriorated, and the rate of economic growth dropped. These problems appeared to confirm the contention that the "limits had been reached for further development within the existing social and political structure."

The discussion of "basic reforms" and "structural changes" became so intense and widespread that the need for such changes became an unquestioned axiom within public opinion. The newspapers gave daily coverage to the issues involved, and consider-

[12] For an account of Brazilian nationalist ideology and its systematic development and promulgation in the ISEB, see Frank Bonilla, "A National Ideology for Development: Brazil," in Kalman H. Silvert (ed.), *Expectant Peoples: Nationalism and Development* (New York, 1964), esp. pp. 237–238.

[13] A good example of the flavor of this discussion is presented in Celso Furtado, *A Pre-Revolução Brasileira* (São Paulo, 1963). Part of this was translated as "Brazil: What Kind of Revolution?" *Foreign Affairs* (July 1963). See also "Fifteen Years of Economic Policy in Brazil," *Economic Bulletin for Latin America*, IX (November 1964), pp. 199–200, for testimony on this debate.

ation of the "basic reforms" took a central place in the political communications process. With the new emphasis on abstract analysis of Brazil's present and future, the specialists in ideologizing, the intelligentsia, assumed a much more important place in politics. Since the late 1940's most Brazilian intellectuals had been nationalists with, as we have seen, a special orientation toward foreign capital. As the intelligentsia received more attention through the heightened ideological discussions, their views on foreign investment had a greater influence on the policy-makers.

"TECHNICAL" PROBLEMS OF FOREIGN INVESTMENT

Just when the priority previously given economic development was being questioned and nationalist ideology was assuming a central place within both the Presidential entourage and elite opinion, the utility of foreign capital for improving the balance-of-payments situation was likewise cast sharply into doubt. In the early 1960's charges for servicing capital imports (both of direct investment and of other forms of capital inflow such as supplier credits) increased markedly, going from approximately 5 percent of all Brazilian foreign-exchange payments in the early 1950's to some 25 percent in the early 1960's.[14] Even more important, capital outflow exceeded annual inflow, so that foreign investment was now perceived as a *drain* rather than an addition to net foreign-exchange resources. This consideration was especially important, for Brazilian economists have considered foreign capital mainly in terms of its effects on the balance of payments.[15]

Furthermore, the attitude of the government *técnicos* was also changing, as they followed the general tide of opinion against foreign capital and as they modified their approach on the basis of the previous period's experience. First, the *técnicos* had seen that foreign investment sometimes led to results they did not like. In particular, foreign firms entering the pharmaceutical and automotive parts industries had often displaced domestic companies, so that firms previously in Brazilian hands were now controlled

[14] "Auge y Declinación del Processo de Sustitución de los Importaciones en el Brasil," *Boletín Económico de América Latina*, XI (March 1964), Table 2. Data for the early 1960's are computed from material in the SUMOC *Boletim*.
[15] See Claude McMillan et al., *International Enterprise in a Developing Economy* (Lansing, Michigan, 1964), pp. 43–50.

by foreign interests. The achievements and experience gained over the previous years had also generated greater self-respect concerning domestic entrepreneurial and technological capacities. Hence the government administrators were reconsidering critically the advantages of importing capital in the form of direct investment in order to obtain foreign managerial and technical know-how. As Raymond Vernon describes a similar development in Mexico, "The time when foreign investors offered their capital and skills in a seller's market has been rapidly passing." [16] Consequently, the government economic administrators did not feel that restricting entry of direct foreign investment would be followed by economic calamity. Indeed, it no longer appeared clear that such investment was promoting the country's economic development; and measures against foreign capital were often recommended because of their alleged advantages for dealing with the accelerated inflation and the balance-of-payments crisis.[17] Thus any "technical" problems that might result from a new policy were easily cleared away.

In these conditions of a nationalist President and entourage hostile to foreign capital and a climate of opinion more interested in "basic reforms" and an "independent foreign policy" than in economic development "per se," the President felt free to promote legislation restricting the entry of direct foreign investment.

Conclusions

In this chapter we have seen some further material on government autonomy in economic policy-making and on one of the principal determinants of its decisions, elite opinion.

First the government was able to shift sharply to a policy of

[16] Raymond Vernon, *The Dilemma of Mexico's Development* (Cambridge, Mass., 1963), p. 173.
[17] Much of the new foreign investment potentially available to Brazil, particularly in the form of direct investment, was tied to equipment imports. Thus it did not constitute foreign exchange available for servicing the country's foreign debt unless it was accompanied by cuts in investment and raw-material imports elsewhere in the economy. Moreover, appalled by the sharp rise and high level of capital charges in the total claims on Brazilian foreign-exchange earnings, government administrators resolved to curtail such charges in the future by reducing present capital inflow.

promoting direct foreign investment, despite the opposition of the leading industrialists and their spokesmen. And when the government did change this policy, it was in response to a new climate of opinion rather than in deference to pressures from organized interest groups.

The whole emphasis which Brazilian policy-making gave to the question of foreign capital after 1960 also indicates a substantial degree of political autonomy. Anyone observing the government's preoccupation with the issue of foreign private investment might have concluded that the country was not faced with other problems—such as accelerating inflation and slackening economic growth—which weighed more heavily on the broader public. (Although nationalist ideologists claimed that measures against foreign investment would help resolve those problems, nothing approaching a rigorous analysis that might substantiate this contention was ever presented.) The fact that this particular problem was selected for policy attention, largely because of its prominence in the political elite's ideology and interpretation of Brazil's needs, suggests a political system relatively free from outside pressures in its choice of policy problems. Albert Hirschman has noted the same phenomenon, and, as he observes,

> Latin American history shows many examples of important actions being taken by the policy-makers without any noticeable pressure from important sectors of public opinion. Recent striking examples [such as] Kubitschek's decision to build Brasília . . . resulted from the policy-makers' more or less autonomous choice rather than from anyone's insistent clamor.[18]

Significantly, Hirschman does not even mention pressure from interest groups or social classes but confines his discussion to "important sectors of public opinion" and access to political communications.

The operation of elite opinion is examined in Chapter 8, but we should note here that once it had shifted far enough in one direction—for example, hostility to foreign investment—it was politically difficult to move far from its bounds. We have also seen how movements in the climate of opinion occur. The Presi-

[18] Albert O. Hirschman, *Journeys toward Progress: Studies of Economic Policy-Making in Latin America* (New York, 1963), pp. 234–235.

dent himself is one of its principal leaders, with considerable freedom in the choice of themes to publicize or ignore. The communications process also has its own internal dynamics, however. These limit the rate at which it can be led, and can determine movements of its own. Once the intelligentsia had begun to stress the need for "basic reforms," the discussion followed its own logic to increasingly more radical positions. This movement within the communications system, in turn, affected all of Brazilian politics.

Finally, the political communications process is by no means a simple reflection of Brazilian reality. It has autonomy in the issues it raises and in the interpretation it gives them. We have already noted the figures concerning the magnitude of foreign capital remissions which were introduced into the discussion and accepted almost unquestioned. Even when such fantastic statistics were not used, the assumption of direct investment's supporters and opponents alike was that the magnitudes involved were large enough to have a determining effect on Brazil's future.

In reality, total foreign investment, and particularly *direct* foreign private investment, have played a relatively small role in Brazilian capital formation and growth. In the periods 1947–1960 and 1955–1960 alike, net foreign capital inflow of all types amounted to approximately 8 percent of all Brazilian fixed investment.[19] Within total capital inflow, *direct* investment was by no means predominant. Even in the years 1955–1960, when it was most important, direct investment was greatly outweighed by supplier credits and came to only one-third of all foreign capital inflow. *Hence less than 3 percent of all Brazilian capital formation was financed by direct foreign investment.* This is hardly a colossal figure even if we make some allowance for direct investment's presumed "qualitative" importance as a complement of imported know-how and managerial resources.[20] The Brazilian political communications process, however, was enough of a closed, self-determining system to proceed in ignorance of such

[19] The figures in this and the subsequent sentence were computed from data in Baer, pp. 232 and 107.
[20] This could be done by considering any additional costs involved in importing technical and administrative know-how in the form of licensing agreements, consultants and expatriates rather than through foreign manufacturing companies.

facts,[21] on its convention that foreign capital was both of enormous proportions and one of the country's most serious policy problems.

This discussion has emphasized the crucial role of the attitudes and perceptions mediating between objective conditions and Brazilian economic policy-makers. Chapter 5 also shows the influence of ideas, and particularly of some widely held economic doctrines.

---

[21] Perhaps because of the blind-spot introduced by ideology, the calculation cited above was not made or publicized in Brazil, and the magnitude of direct foreign investment was usually discussed in terms of the larger amounts of *total* foreign capital inflow.

Export Policy

Export policy provides another example of the political autonomy of Brazilian economic policy-making. As we will see, policy here was made in direct opposition to the interests of major private groups, the exporters and the landed elites producing primary products, in deference instead to doctrines which commanded widespread influence among the government administrators and in elite opinion.

Brazilian Export Performance

In previous chapters we saw the importance of Brazil's continuing balance-of-payments problem in conditioning the country's policy toward protection, allocation decisions, and direct foreign investment. This situation reflected the failure of Brazil's exports to grow proportionately with aggregate output and domestic demand. In fact, exports stand out as perhaps the only major exception to the general pattern of rapid, across-the-board growth in Brazil. In a period when almost all indices of economic development—agricultural output, electricity generation, educational enrollments—rose very dynamically, exports were virtually stagnant. Between 1947–1949 and 1960–1962, when GNP expanded 140 percent, total export earnings increased only 13 percent.[1]

[1] Throughout this discussion, 1947–1949 and 1960–1962 are used as the points of reference. The year 1962 is the cutoff point, because 1963 and 1964 were years of relative recession in the Brazilian economy, and the slackening of internal demand affected normal exports. The figures cited in this and subsequent paragraphs were computed from indices published in *Conjuntura Econômica;* from data in Werner Baer, *Industrialization and Economic Development in Brazil* (Homewood, Ill., 1965) pp. 36–37, 40, 71,

It is at first sight surprising that Brazilian exports did not do better during this period, either as a result of government policies promoting exports to deal with the balance-of-payments problem or as a result of market forces and the persistent fall in the dollar-cruzeiro exchange rate which the situation engendered.[2] Let us therefore consider the factors affecting Brazilian exports. We can discuss them in terms of the two principal commodity groups: coffee, which accounted for some 42 percent of all Brazilian export earnings in the late 1940's and 55 percent in the early 1960's; and a large number of noncoffee primary products, the so-called "minor exports"—cocoa, cotton, tobacco, iron ore, sugar, hides, rubber, timber, and meat.

Brazil's coffee exports have been conditioned by the country's valorization policy. As noted in Chapter 2, in an effort to maximize the foreign-exchange earnings from coffee, the Brazilian government has bought or sold coffee stocks, depending on conditions in the world market. As a result of this policy, world coffee prices have probably been higher than they would otherwise have been. Because of the high prices maintained, however, and because of Brazil's dominant position in the market and consequent willingness to accept the role of residual supplier, Brazil's share in world coffee trade has declined drastically: from 76 percent in the first decade of the century, to 53 percent in 1934–1938, to approximately 38 percent of the early 1960's.[3] And as a result of this policy, the increment in world demand has gone to other producers, and the quantum of Brazilian exports remained almost stationary through the postwar period.[4] For this reason and because the often-cited price inelasticity of world coffee demand actually applies only in the short run and in the aggregate—that is, not to individual suppliers—the policy has

272; and from *Yearbook of International Trade Statistics, 1963* (United Nations, 1965).

[2] Data on this depreciation, as the external devaluation of the cruzeiro proceeded more rapidly than the internal inflation, are presented in Nathaniel H. Leff, "Export Stagnation and Autarkic Development in Brazil, 1947–62," *Quarterly Journal of Economics* (May 1967).

[3] These figures are from Antônio Delfim Netto, *O Problema do Café no Brasil* (São Paulo, 1959), p. 159; and Baer, p. 39.

[4] Computed from data in Baer, p. 277.

been sharply criticized.[5] It is not clear, however, that these criticisms are justified. In all such discussion of optimal long-run versus short-run policies, choice of the discount rate for evaluating future gains is crucial. The criticisms of Brazil's "short-sightedness" usually imply a zero discount rate. In fact, the coffee market seems to approximate the oligopolist model analyzed by George Stigler, in which one firm has so large a share of the market that it maximizes profits with a high-price strategy, even though this encourages new entrants and subsequently reduces the dominant firm's market share.[6]

In reality, although Brazil's export troubles are generally attributed to coffee, the dollar value of coffee exports *rose* 34 percent during this period. The poor performance of the country's aggregate export earnings resulted largely from the behavior of *noncoffee* exports. Between 1947–1949 and 1960–1962, the value of these exports declined 4 percent, and, as noted earlier, their contribution to total foreign-exchange earnings fell.

Neither stagnant world demand nor sharply declining prices account for Brazil's poor export performance. World trade in these products increased at an average annual rate of 3.1 percent during this period;[7] and international prices for Brazil's noncoffee exports fell approximately 8 percent between 1947–1949 and 1960–1962. The volume Brazil exported, however, rose a mere 7 percent during the entire period.[8] This quantum stagnation derived from a decline in the proportion of primary-product exportables that were sold on the world market rather than

[5] Another, more radical criticism of Brazilian coffee policy is that the country should adopt a low-price policy both to encourage habit formation and increase the growth of world demand (Netto, p. 328), and to increase Brazil's share in the world market by driving out or forestalling the entry of other producers. The success of such a policy would depend on the relative efficiency and comparative advantage of Brazil and its competitors in Latin America and Africa. Other criticisms relate to the inefficiency of the government's coffee inventory policy even within its goal of oligopolistic market strategy. This was discussed in Chapter 2.

[6] George Stigler, *The Theory of Price* (New York, 1952), pp. 232–234.

[7] This is the average rate at which the quantum of cotton, rubber, cocoa, sugar, and tobacco increased in world trade during the 1950's. Data are from Baer, p. 40 (Table 3-5-A).

[8] Both price and volume trends were computed from *Conjuntura Econômica*, indices 84, 70.

diverted to domestic consumption. Between 1947 and 1961, Brazilian agricultural output expanded dynamically, at an annual cumulative rate over 4 percent. The share of exports in total agricultural output, however, fell almost 50 percent.[9]

Why did Brazil's exports of products other than coffee fail to do better? The immediate answer is the exchange-rate policy that was followed.[10] As stated earlier, the exchange rate for exports was initially overvalued in an effort to avoid a decline in world coffee prices; and it was subsequently adjusted only with considerable lags to the country's internal inflation. These measures reducing the price competitiveness of Brazil's products on international markets can explain the poor export performance. The real question, however, is *why* such policies were followed. The Brazilian authorities have shown considerable ingenuity in manipulation of multiple *import* exchange rates, and had they wanted, they could have displayed similar flexibility in a consistent effort to promote noncoffee exports.

Rather, it appears that the government's economic administrators approached Brazil's long-term postwar economic prospects with a strong bias against exportation, either as a source of aggregate growth or as a means of dealing with the country's balance-of-payments problems.[11] First there was considerable pessimism concerning the possibilities of expanding exports, because of the low income-elasticity of world demand for most primary products. Elasticity pessimism was especially pervasive concerning coffee—and may indeed have influenced the decision to operate with a short-term horizon in this market—but it affected thinking about other exports as well.

Government officials were also concerned with the instability and risks of depending on exportation as a source of income and supply. The drastic decline in export earnings during the world depression and the difficulties of import supply during World

[9] Output and exports computed from data in Baer, pp. 71 (Table 3-11-B), 37 (Table 3-2-B).

[10] For a discussion of Brazilian exchange-rate policy in the period 1947–1953, see Donald Huddle, "Furtado on Exchange Control and Economic Development: An Evaluation and Reinterpretation of the Brazilian Case," *Economic Development and Cultural Change*, XV (April 1967).

[11] The following material is based on interviews with civil servants and former officials in the Export Division of the *Banco do Brasil*, the Monetary Authority, and the Development Bank.

War II had left a deep impression, and in effect the authorities discounted export earnings by a large risk factor.[12] In contrast with dependence on international conditions beyond their control, development of domestic production capacity for many goods previously imported seemed a straightforward solution to the country's balance-of-payments and supply problems. By the early 1950's these considerations were reinforced by ideological currents stressing the importance of import substitution and industrial development as a means to modernization and emancipation from colonial dependence on the world economy. As in other Latin American countries which had had similar experiences, the emphasis was on "inward-looking" growth. Still, as suggested below, import substitution might well have been compatible with expanded exports. Here, however, another factor intervened: the government's approach to international trade in products other than coffee.

From interviews with Brazilian economic administrators, as well as from a detailed study of Brazilian export policy,[13] it is clear that the government approached export possibilities with an implicit "exportable surplus" theory of trade. Indeed, this attitude was sometimes made completely explicit, as in published work by the chief administrator of CACEX (Carteira de Comércio Exterior), the export licensing authority, between 1954 and 1961.[14] According to this doctrine, a country exports only the "surplus" which is "left over" after the domestic market for the commodity has been "adequately" supplied. Domestic demand takes priority, however, and must be supplied *even if internal prices are lower than world market prices.* This pre-comparative advantage approach seems to have been adopted in Brazil largely because of the naive intuitive appeal of the doctrine that a coun-

[12] Cyclical or random disturbances seem to have been more in the minds of the Brazilian officials than a long-term deterioration in the terms of trade for primary-product exporters.

[13] See Ivan Lakos, "The Effects of Brazil's Foreign Exchange Policy on the Value of Her Exports and on the Flow of Private Foreign Investment with Respect to Brazil's Economic Development" (Ph.D. dissertation, Harvard University, 1962), esp. Chapter 3. I am grateful to Donald Huddle for bringing this reference to my attention.

[14] Tosta Filho, *Fatores Estructurais e Conjunturais do Comércio Exterior* (Banco do Brasil: Rio de Janeiro, 1958). This reference is cited and discussed in detail by Lakos.

try produces primarily for its own needs and that the exports are only what is "left over." [15] An effort to reduce the effects of rising export prices on domestic consumers was also present.

The "surplus" approach to trade was followed by the Brazilian authorities throughout this period. In order to ensure that the domestic market was adequately supplied, exports were discouraged and internal prices for exportable goods were held down by overvaluing the exchange rate for noncoffee products. When these measures were not sufficient, export quotas and outright prohibitions on primary-product exports—and occasionally on would-be manufactured exports [16]—were also imposed unless there was clear indication that the domestic market was being "adequately" supplied. According to the rule followed, export licenses were denied if the export commodity's internal price was rising.[17] This criterion was often met. As a result, export licenses were frequently denied, leading to the diversion of exportable production to the domestic market, and to the stagnation of the export quantum that we have noted.

The exportable-surplus approach to trade had two other dynamic features which limited output and exportation.[18] First, the stipulation that domestic demand had to be served, even if internal prices were lower than world market levels, led to lower domestic prices than would otherwise have developed. Hence, if domestic demand was at all price-elastic, the "needs" of the internal market became so much greater, and the "exportable

---

[15] Brazil has not been the only less developed country to follow this approach to exportation. The assumptions underlying this policy are discussed in my paper "The 'Exportable Surplus' Approach to Foreign Trade in Underdeveloped Countries", *Economic Development and Cultural Change*, 1968.

[16] Stanley Stein, *The Brazilian Cotton Manufacture* (Cambridge, Mass., 1957), pp. 169–170, 172–173, discusses the government prohibition of textile exports in 1945–1946. Claude McMillan, *International Enterprise in a Developing Economy* (Lansing, Mich., 1964), p. 114, mentions a similar episode when the government denied an export license to an automobile manufacturer in 1959.

[17] The original provision which provided for export prohibitions stipulated that exports could be permitted after the domestic market had been supplied with 107 percent of its previous year's consumption. This was later abandoned, however, if the authorities saw the need for greater restrictions: e.g., for inventory accumulation or simply if prices were rising (Lakos, p. 141).

[18] These points are also discussed in Lakos, pp. 133–141.

surplus" so much smaller. The impact of international demand on domestic price formation, and thus on investment and production plans, was also restricted. Consequently, unless supply of these products was completely price-inelastic, production was also lower than it would otherwise be. Exports suffered on both accounts; for they were determined as a residual of output (which this approach restricts) and domestic consumption (which it encourages). That exports were not choked off completely under this policy is an indication of Brazil's strong competitive position in these products. Indeed, Brazilian producers were sufficiently competitive so that even with the overvalued exchange rate, the government had to resort to quantitative controls in order to restrict exports of these products.

This policy also had other pernicious consequences, for example, in increasing the dependence of Brazilian exports on one product, coffee.[19] One important property particularly affected the whole pattern of Brazilian development during the postwar period. By contributing to the stagnation of exports, the policy led to the persistent Brazilian balance-of-payments problem. During the 1950's this led to a steady depreciation of the dollar-cruzeiro exchange rate for imports. These devaluations did not, however, lead to payments equilibration by the normal twofold mechanism of making Brazilian exports more competitive on world markets and making imports more expensive in Brazilian currency. Because of the policy barriers to exportation, *devaluation could have effects only on the import side,* and the whole burden of adjustment was placed on import substitution. With domestic income growing much more rapidly than exports and import supply, this led to a process of self-sustained import substitution. The development of domestic production in one industry after another provoked by the continuing balance-of-payments problem probably went too far, however, in the sense that many import-substitute products could have been acquired more economically through exportation and foreign trade than through domestic manufacture.[20]

[19] Leff, "The 'Exportable Surplus' Approach."
[20] This is discussed in Leff, "Export Stagnation and Autarkic Development."

The Informational Requirements for
Effective Policy-Making

By restricting their access to world markets and reducing internal prices for their output, the exportable-surplus policy went directly against the interests of the landed elites producing Brazil's primary products. This is another example of the Brazilian government's relative freedom from political constraints in economic policy-making.[21] Even a sympathetic study of the export policy concludes, however, that its effects on the country's trade and development were extremely harmful.[22] As this indicates, political autonomy is not a sufficient condition for the formulation of effective policy promoting economic development. Certain informational prerequisites, in the sense of both accurate data and well-conceived analysis, must be met as well. The discussion in Chapter 2 of the conditions that led the government to set overly high internal coffee prices provided an example of policy based on poor data. The "surplus" approach to trade and some of the other doctrines which underlay Brazil's export policies offer instances of unexamined (and sometimes mistaken) assumptions which conditioned fundamental policy orientations.

One important example may be seen in the general pessimism concerning primary-product exports. This attitude, based on the doctrine of the low per capita income-elasticity of demand for primary products, may have been rational in the early postwar years, after the experience of the world depression. With population (and income) in the developed countries growing rapidly during the 1950's, however, the corollary of stagnant world mar-

---

[21] It may be suggested that the "surplus" export policy was adopted in deference to the interest of the industrialists in lowering the cost of their raw materials. They certainly supported the policy, but as noted earlier, it was also applied to finished manufactured products. An effort at reducing the impact of rising export prices on domestic consumers may have been present to a limited degree, though Brazilian governments have not hesitated to enact measures in monetary and fiscal policy which had much greater inflationary effects. An anti-inflationary effort may be the main reason underlying the "surplus" policy in other countries; but in Brazil, it seems to have been adopted mainly because of the doctrine's naive intuitive appeal.

[22] Leff, "The 'Exportable Surplus' Approach."

kets for primary products no longer held. What is worth noting is the long lag before feedback from experience and from readily available data on demographic trends in the advanced countries modified these orientations. As late as 1962, the doctrine was repeated by a leading Brazilian economist in the government's economic plan. This appeared together with statistics which showed that in the 1950's, exports (excluding petroleum) of other Latin American countries had been increasing more than twice as rapidly as Brazil's noncoffee exports! [23]

Another example of the policy-making process' failure to generate and act upon relevant information occurred in connection with the presumed instability of export earnings. By the late 1950's it was clear that cyclical fluctuations in the advanced countries had become relatively rare and mild. Consequently, the risk of sharp declines in export earnings which might result from conditions beyond Brazil's control had been reduced. Furthermore, because of the diversion of output to the domestic market, the share of exports in the sectors producing exportable products had declined to a relatively low level. For almost all the "minor products"—cotton, sugar, tobacco, rubber, leather, and beef—the export coefficient was considerably below the figure, say, 20 percent, which an exporting country might rationally consider undue dependence on foreign trade. At the same time, the share of noncoffee exports in Brazilian GNP had been reduced to 3.2 percent, so that the possible impact of export fluctuations on aggregate income was also diminished. Brazilian policy-makers did not, however, notice these changes, and they failed to modify their policies accordingly.

A similar failure to reexamine once rational policies in light of changing circumstances may have occurred in the case of coffee. As noted earlier, Brazil's oligopolist policy in the world coffee market may have been justified as a means of maximizing the country's foreign-exchange earnings. The valorization programs in the first decades of the century were acclaimed a success even by critics who had first denounced them on laissez-faire grounds. Coffee prices were supported, and, taking into account the costs of retention (which had been financed by a loan from English

---

[23] *Plano Trienal de Desenvolvimento Econômico e Social* (Rio de Janeiro, 1962), pp. 34–37.

bankers), the São Paulo government had still been able to realize a large profit on its coffee inventories.[24] The debacle of 1930 came as a consequence of the collapse of demand in the world depression—an event which Brazil had understandably not foreseen. In this perspective, Brazil must indeed be credited for its activist orientation and innovating ability in attempting to control its environment and better its economic position.

By the middle 1950's, however, when Brazil's share in world coffee exports had declined so drastically, a reconsideration of the policy was in order. Such a review might have considered the advantages of alternative policies, under different assumptions concerning the value of foreign exchange, alternative projections of future market and cost conditions, with different discount rates to evaluate varying short- and long-run gains. It is not clear what such an analysis would have concluded. The point is, however, that the policy-makers did not undertake it. Impressed by the relative success of the policy in earlier years and mesmerized by the doctrine of the price-inelasticity of world coffee demand, government administrators did not consider new perspectives. Again, this doctrinal inertia within the policy-making system was not forced by political pressures. The coffee planters had long been calling for a low-price, high-volume export policy, which would wipe out foreign competition and increase Brazil's share in the world coffee market.[25]

Finally, Brazilian export policy provides another example of how harmful economic policy decisions may be made not because of political distortions—for example, pressures which induce the policy-makers to "maximize the wrong variable" [26]—but simply because of poor technical analysis. The general framework within which the balance-of-payments issue was approached had serious conceptual deficiencies which prevented the government from optimizing even for the goals it set for itself.

The foreign-exchange problem was formulated as a choice between export promotion and import substitution; and for reasons

[24] Netto, pp. 61–153.
[25] See the speeches of Salvio de Almeida Prado, long-time head of the São Paulo coffee planters' association (FARESP), in *Dez Anos na Política do Café* (São Paulo, 1956), pp. 208–215.
[26] Charles P. Kindleberger, *Economic Development* (Second Edition, New York, 1965), pp. 127–130.

previously discussed, export promotion was rejected. Because of the "either/or" framework used, expanded exports were not given serious consideration even as a partial solution to the country's foreign-exchange problem. There were no good technical reasons why such a dichotomous approach had to be applied, however. Indeed, other analysis has suggested that under Brazil's conditions of elastic factor supply, output of primary-product exports could have been expanded *simultaneously* with high rates of industrial development and import substitution.[27] A model in which, especially with high tariffs, industrial import substitution goes together with expanding primary-product exportation—with the latter generating demand and imported inputs for the former—is certainly conceivable. The rapid industrial development of São Paulo stimulated by the coffee boom at the turn of the century is indeed a good example.[28] This experience was forgotten, however, and in the postwar period the government administrators did not perceive that export expansion and import substitution could be complementary rather than competitive courses. If they had, the foreign-exchange problem would have been considerably mitigated; and the higher rate of primary-product expansion *and* of industrial development would have permitted even more rapid aggregate growth.[29]

The point of this discussion is not that in Brazil, as in other countries, decision-makers sometimes found erroneous conceptions appealing; it is rather the extent to which such doctrines actually prevailed in the Brazilian policy-making process and the long lag before they were corrected. What is noteworthy is not that policy-makers found the "surplus" approach to trade intu-

[27] Leff, "Export Stagnation and Autarkic Development," Section IV.

[28] Nathaniel H. Leff, "Note on Brazilian Economic Development before 1939" (mimeo, 1967).

[29] Carlos F. Díaz-Alejandro reaches a similar conclusion in his analysis of postwar Argentine economic growth: industrial development would also have been more rapid if rates of agricultural exportation had been higher. See his "An Interpretation of Argentine Economic Growth since 1930: Part II," *Journal of Development Studies*, III, 174 (January 1967). Hla Myint has also emphasized the complementarity between export expansion and import substitution. See his interpretation of the contrasting postwar experiences of Burma and Indonesia on the one hand, and Malaya, Thailand, and the Philippines on the other. This is to be found in his "The Inward and Outward Looking Countries of Southeast Asia," *The Malayan Economic Review*, (April 1967).

itively convincing, but that an analysis of the doctrine's harmful effects was not formulated, and it continued to influence policy. Similarly, the delay in feedback before data on world trade modified the pessimism concerning export possibilities is truly impressive. In Chapter 10 we will consider the intellectual environment which made possible these informational and analytical deficiencies in the policy-making process.

In the preceding four chapters we have assembled data on postwar Brazilian economic policy and singled out some important features of the decision-making process. We can now draw some general conclusions concerning economic policy-making and postwar Brazilian development and then we turn to an analysis of the political structure within which it took place.

CHAPTER 6

Economic Policy-Making and Postwar Brazilian Development

We can now bring together material from the previous chapters to present the main features of postwar Brazilian economic growth.[1] As Table 16 indicates, aggregate real output in Brazil

TABLE 16. *Growth of Real Output in Brazil, 1947–1964*

Year	Annual Percentage Increase	Three-Year Moving Average
1947	8.0	—
1948	9.5	7.6%
1949	5.6	6.7
1950	5.0	5.2
1951	5.1	5.2
1952	5.6	4.6
1953	3.2	3.3
1954	7.7	5.9
1955	6.8	5.2
1956	1.9	5.2
1957	6.9	5.1
1958	6.6	6.9
1959	7.3	6.9
1960	6.7	7.1
1961	7.3	6.5
1962	5.4	4.8
1963	1.6	3.4
1964	3.1	—

Source. Fundação Getúlio Vargas.

[1] These paragraphs also draw upon material documented in my studies, "Export Stagnation and Autarkic Development in Brazil, 1947–1962," *Quarterly Journal of Economics* (May 1967); "Import Constraints and

grew at a relatively high rate.[2] Between 1947 and 1964, the average annual increase was 5.7 percent.

We can discuss this growth in terms of the two principal features of Brazilian economic development in the postwar period. First, aggregate demand grew at extremely rapid rates, both because of rising real income and because of excess demand, reflected in the inflation.[3] Second, because of relatively elastic domestic supply conditions, part of this rising demand could be transformed into higher real output.

We should note that Brazilian agriculture proved responsive to the expanding market. Between 1946–1947 and 1962–1963, output of food and of agricultural commodities for the internal market (i.e., excluding coffee) increased at an annual cumulative rate of 4.6 percent.[4] This supply permitted an approximate balance, in aggregate terms, with the rising demand for agricultural commodities.[5]

Development: Causes of the Recent Decline of Brazilian Economic Growth," *Review of Economics and Statistics*, (November 1967); with Antônio Delfim Netto, "Import Substitution, Foreign Investment and International Disequilibrium in Brazil," *Journal of Development Studies*, (April 1966); and Chapters 6, 5, 3, and 2 of *The Brazilian Capital Goods Industry, 1929–1964* (Cambridge, Mass., 1968).

[2] Real output in Brazil is estimated by the semi-official Fundação Getúlio Vargas. The series is a weighted average, using a moving base, of several sectoral indices for which physical data—for example, on electricity generation—are available. For details, see Werner Baer, *Industrialization and Economic Development in Brazil* (Homewood, Ill., 1965), pp. 218–221. The Fundação states in its tables that real output is computed in constant 1949 prices.

[3] Between 1948 and 1958, the GDP deflator rose at an average annual rate of 13 percent, and between 1959 and 1964, at 50 percent. The sources of the Brazilian inflation are discussed in Chapter 9.

[4] Computed from indices 38 and 39 in *Conjuntura Econômica*. The year 1963 was used as the cut-off point because that was the last year for which the *Conjuntura Econômica* indices were available at the time of writing. Another time-series of agricultural production, prepared by the Brazilian Institute for Geography and Statistics (IBGE) with the output figures for 46 agricultural products, shows an annual cumulative growth rate of 4.5 between 1954–1955 and 1963–1964, the series' initial and terminal points. See IBGE, *Anuário Estatístico do Brasil—1966* (Rio de Janeiro, 1967), p. 68. Brazilian agricultural development during this period is examined in Antônio Delfim Netto et al., *Problemas Econômicas da Agricultura Brasileira* (São Paulo, 1965).

[5] Excluding 1963 and 1964, when Brazilian development slackened, the long-term rate of growth of income was 6 percent. Assuming an income-elastic-

The supply of imports, however, did not increase proportionately with domestic money income and demand. In an effort to deal with the ensuing balance-of-payments problem, Brazilian policy-makers promoted the domestic production of many goods previously imported, in an attempt to reduce the demand for foreign exchange. Since most Brazilian imports consisted of manufactured goods, promotion of import substitution was equivalent to support for accelerated industrialization. With buoyant aggregate demand and a marginal propensity to import which did not decline during the period, however, import substitution led only to a changing composition of imports, while the international imbalance continued. The persistent demand pressures on the exchange market were reflected in an upward trend, in real terms, in the cruzeiro-dollar rate for imports.[6] As a result, quite apart from government protectionist measures, relative prices moved to favor domestic producers for many products previously imported. With income-elastic supply of factors such as capital, entrepreneurship, and skilled labor, industrial output responded with an annual cumulative growth rate of 8.8 percent. This resulted in a process of rapid growth led by industrial development until 1963, when the income-inelasticity of import supply became so great as to constrain aggregate Brazilian growth.[7]

Economic Policy in Brazilian Economic Development

The place of government policy in this process is clear. The rapid growth in aggregate demand and the diversion of this demand from overseas to domestic producers stemmed from the inflation, and from the bias against exports and the resulting inadequacy of import supply. At the same time, the government moved to provide important external economies—such as roads for agricul-

---

ity for food of 0.7, demand was rising at an annual rate of approximately 4.2 percent, in rough balance with the output figure given. Data in John W. Mellor, *The Economics of Agricultural Development* (Ithaca, N.Y., 1966), pp. 63–64, suggest an income-elasticity of demand for food of 0.6, which would indicate an even more favorable situation.

[6] This reflected the fact that, as mentioned earlier, the cruzeiro's external depreciation proceeded more rapidly than the internal inflation.

[7] The slowdown of Brazilian growth after 1962 is discussed in Chapter 10.

ture [8]—and to overcome indivisibilities in domestic manufacturing supply—notably steel—which might have inhibited growth.

It is difficult to draw conclusions concerning the quality of Brazilian economic policy-making, but some evidence suggests that, in general and with the major exception of exports, it may well have played a positive role in the country's development. Brazil's high rate of growth during the period is at least some indication that government action did not paralyze the economy. Moreover, the growth rate did not slacken during the 1950's, despite the vastly expanded public-sector role in capital formation and in allocation and production activities. As the case of export policy indicates, Brazilian development did not follow an optimal pattern and involved unnecessary costs in sacrificing opportunities offered by trade and comparative advantage. Still, we must recognize that until the end of the period, Brazilian national income grew at high rates computed on the basis of 1949 prices.

Furthermore, not only did Brazilian development proceed at relatively high rates, but it was also relatively stable. The standard deviation of the annual growth rate was less than 10 percent away from the annual average. This contrasts with the experience of Argentina, for example, where policy-makers were much less effective in maintaining steady growth, and the standard deviation was more than twice the annual average.[9]

In spite of the respectable rates of growth achieved in the postwar years—and indeed since the turn of the century—Brazilian per capita income was still relatively low, approximately $300, at the end of this period.[10] This indicates the difficulty of achieving economic progress when a country starts from poor initial conditions, particularly when population is growing at 2 to 3 per-

[8] I am indebted to Gordon W. Smith for discussion of the effects of road construction on agricultural marketing and production in Brazil. Some of this material is contained in his "Agricultural Marketing and Economic Development: A Brazilian Case Study" (Ph.D. dissertation, Harvard University, 1965).

[9] The figure for Argentina is from Geoffrey Maynard and Willy Van Rijckeghem, "Stabilization Policy in an Inflationary Economy: Argentina" (mimeo, 1966), p. 1. The figure for Brazil was computed from Table 16.

[10] Material on earlier Brazilian economic development is presented in my paper, "Note on Brazilian Economic Development before 1939" (mimeo, 1967). The paper also examines the reasons for the low level of Brazilian per capita income in 1900, and attributes this to the poor performance of Brazilian exports during most of the nineteenth century.

cent annually. The problem facing Brazilian policy-makers, however, was maintaining satisfactory *rates* of growth to move beyond these low levels. In this effort, despite the errors we have noted, the country did demonstrate a creditable performance.

As suggested in Chapter 2, protection served as the functional equivalent of a selective devaluation on the import side. The emphasis on the "basic industries" stemmed from an implicit model of economic growth hampered by a rising real cost of imports. This approach was indeed justified by events, for the cost of imports in domestic resources rose through most of the 1950's. As indicated in our discussion of export policy, this cost rise was in part a problem the policy-makers had themselves created. But they were at least able to deal constructively with some of its consequences, and helped spare Brazil from the worst of both worlds—stagnation in foreign trade *and* in domestic production.

Even the decision in 1962 to restrict direct foreign private investment may not have been as catastrophic as sometimes alleged.[11] It is not clear that for a country like Brazil, this particular form of capital inflow is more advantageous than others, such as supplier credits. In any case, as noted at the end of Chapter 4, even in the years when direct investment was most important, it was only of minor significance in Brazilian capital formation and was much overshadowed by commercial loans.[12]

There is also some indirect evidence that the government's allocation policies may have been, on the whole, well conceived. During the postwar period, the marginal capital-output ratio showed no tendency to rise.[13] This is the more noteworthy since these years saw a sharp increase in the share of the government in

[11] See, for example, Baer, pp. 199–200.

[12] It should be added that the net contribution of foreign capital inflow to aggregate investment resources in an underdeveloped country is not clear. Hollis Chenery and Peter Eckstein have shown that for most Latin American countries in the 1950's, domestic saving and foreign capital inflow were *inversely* related. See their "Development Alternatives for Latin America," *Journal of Political Economy*, forthcoming, Table A-5.

[13] This point has also been noted by Werner Baer, "Brazil: Inflation and Economic Efficiency," *Economic Development and Cultural Change*, XI (November 1963). Data on the marginal capital-output ratio in Brazil, 1947–1960, are presented in Banco Nacional de Desenvolvimento Econômico, *XII Exposição sôbre o Programa de Reaparelhamento Econômico* (Rio de Janeiro, 1964), pp. 10–11.

total fixed capital formation; and the public sector's investments were directed overwhelmingly to areas of high *sectoral* capital-output ratios—roads, railways, petroleum refining, electricity generation, and steel. The fact that the aggregate capital-output ratio did not rise despite the pronounced shift in the sectoral composition of investment suggests that these investments may have been well directed, and that they succeeded, as intended, in breaking bottlenecks and raising the productivity of investment elsewhere in the economy.

Before concluding our evaluation of Brazilian economic policy, however, we should consider other areas where the picture may be less favorable. First, the recurrent balance-of-payments crises. These were less an indication of "national bankruptcy" than of a supply of imports that was not increasing as rapidly as internal demand. The shortage of foreign exchange did lead to investment distortions, however, and after 1962 this shortage caused a slackening in aggregate growth. Since the insufficient supply of imports stemmed from the export policies discussed in Chapter 5, this case exemplifies the pernicious consequences that ill-conceived doctrines had on Brazilian economic policy and development, but not the effects of *political* constraints.

Brazilian economic policy has also been condemned because of the country's persistent inflation. As we have seen, the Brazilian government did demonstrate the capacity to raise the share of its tax revenues in GNP to a level that is relatively high by international standards. A later chapter discusses the reasons for the large budget deficits in terms of certain structural features of Brazilian politics, not the government's political weakness. We should note, moreover, that it is not clear the inflation had negative effects on Brazil's development. For one thing, unlike some underdeveloped countries which have followed overly orthodox fiscal and monetary policies, Brazilian growth has rarely been constrained by insufficient aggregate demand. Furthermore, on the supply side, an econometric study of the Brazilian inflation has concluded that the rate of investment was positively related with the rate of price increase; [14] while some of the usual distor-

---

[14] H. W. Odeh, *The Impact of Inflation on the Level of Economic Activity* (Rotterdam, 1964), pp. 81–91.

tions that inflation might have been expected to induce in investment allocations did not in fact appear.[15]

It is not suggested that Brazilian decision-makers always chose the policies making the maximum contribution to economic growth. We have noted examples of errors and of missed opportunities for even higher rates of growth. These instances, however, should not detract from the favorable overall picture.

The generally favorable effects of Brazilian economic policy may have been due to luck—a fortuitous correspondence on some points between the economic ideology that influenced policy-making and the country's objective conditions. The main point in the present context, however, is that *the government was often trying to promote economic development, and that political pressures did not prevent it from proceeding with policies it believed were well conceived for reaching this goal.* This leads to our next point, the government's effectiveness, both politically and administratively, in implementing its decisions.

Politics and Brazilian Economic Policy

Our discussion in the Introduction raised several questions about politics and economic development, concerning particularly the policy-makers' interest in development and their effectiveness in proceeding in that direction despite partisan pressures, political instability, and other conditions that might inhibit effective decision-making. The early chapters, particularly the material on allocation decisions, indicated the Brazilian authorities' desire for economic development as they conceived it, and their emphasis on policy measures which they believed would promote growth. In practice, many of the political conditions that might have been expected to hamper effective policy-making were also overcome.

We stressed earlier the impressive growth of the public sector's share in national income and in investment and the government's ability to direct resources to the industries, largely within the public sector, where it thought they would do the most good. The influence of domestic "vested interests" or

---

[15] Baer, "Brazil: Inflation and Economic Efficiency."

"selfish elites" was slight. Similarly, the government was able to implement decisions that overseas interests opposed vigorously, such as establishment of the Petrobrás oil company and the exclusion of direct foreign investment. This record does not indicate a government too weak politically to formulate and execute effective policies.

It may be suggested the landed elites constituted a major exception to this pattern. Throughout the period, government policy did relatively little in the area of agriculture, and the absence of land reform has been cited as evidence of the continuing political dominance of the landlords.

Our discussion of coffee policy pointed out that the planters have been superseded as an important group in Brazilian economic policy-making. Similarly, the "surplus" export policy went directly against the interests of the landowners involved in production of other primary products. More generally, one reason why policy-makers did relatively little in agrarian policy is that, as noted earlier, in most areas Brazilian agriculture performed well during the postwar period. Hence agriculture never appeared to constitute a bottleneck for growth. Perhaps even more important within the Brazilian system of policy-making, the modernizing ideology which exercised so crucial an influence accorded little importance to agriculture for national modernization. Since industry—and particularly heavy industry—was considered the key problem for the country's development, it is not surprising that more was not done for agriculture.[16]

In addition to its general political effectiveness, the government also had available the instruments to carry out its decisions. Although much has been said of the inefficiency of Brazil's civil service, the fact remains that the large increases in tax revenue *were* collected, and the large government investment projects

[16] In the early 1960's, new ideological currents did bring the question of land reform to the forefront of attention. Land reform is a major undertaking into which no government enters lightly, however, because of the possibility that disruption of food supply may lead to famine in the cities. Consideration of the issue was also hampered because it was caught up in the maneuvering that accompanied the country's deep constitutional crisis of 1962–1964 (see Chapter 10). The groups whose opposition brought the Goulart regime's deposition were the urban middle strata of São Paulo and Belo Horizonte, and the military, which in Brazil has not been considered the political representative of the landlords.

were implemented without any debacles.[17] The staffing of the vastly expanded public—and private—sectors, moreover, was carried out without abundant resources of "high-level manpower."[18]

The government was able to proceed with the limited educational and administrative resources available, largely through effective manipulation of a few key economic parameters: the exchange rate and hence marginal supply conditions and relative prices in much of the economy; the supply of domestic credits and long-term investment resources through the *Banco do Brasil* and the National Development Bank; and the supply of imports and foreign credits. Apart from their own quantitative importance, these resources were highly complementary with other inputs, so that the government could exert considerable leverage on domestic investment and production plans.

Our discussion also suggests that the importance of corruption in influencing policy formulation and administration has been greatly exaggerated. Despite all the talk about "Brazilians not paying their taxes," tax collections grew rapidly and reached an impressive level. And the main determinant of government allocation decisions was nationalist ideology and its perceptions of the "objective" needs of the situation, rather than corruption. *Within the framework* of the government's major decisions—for example, the commitment to import-substituting industrialization, allocating equipment imports and domestic investment resources for "basic industries"—graft and personal connections

[17] It should be noted that the picture of Brazilian administration as spectacularly inefficient or paper-shuffling comes from areas other than the new institutions established for investment and production activities in the postwar period.

[18] The illiteracy rate in Brazil during this period was approximately 50 percent, and the percentage of university students within the population was relatively small, 0.13 percent in the 1950's. This put Brazil far behind many other poor countries—for example, Argentina, Egypt, Greece, Colombia, Portugal, Spain, Mexico, and Turkey. (Data are from Bruce Russet et al., *World Handbook of Political and Social Indicators*, (New Haven, 1964, pp. 214–215). Generally, in terms of international comparisons of human resource availability, Brazil ranks very low. In the composite educational stock index developed by Frederick Harbison and Charles Myers, for example, *Education, Manpower, and Economic Growth* (New York, 1964), p. 33, Brazil ranks as "partially developed" and is twenty-sixth from the bottom of the 75 countries considered.

may have sometimes been influential. This, however, only affected policy "in the small," whereas policy in the large was determined by the very different considerations of the process described earlier. The political-gossip approach to Brazilian economic policy-making, however, does not distinguish the major decisions from the minor ones. This approach also fails to perceive that the scope for personal influence may be limited within a broader policy framework (of which it is largely unaware), in which issues are formulated and resolved according to very different criteria.

More generally, serious administrative corruption may also be less important than is sometimes suggested; for the Monetary Authority and the National Development Bank, which made many of the important allocation decisions, have a universal reputation for being staffed with professional "technicians" against whom the accusation of grafting has rarely been raised. Indeed, in cases where use of material incentives to influence political behavior clearly did occur, it generally went from the government to the private sector rather than vice versa! As noted, the government sometimes used public-sector loans or favorable import terms to quiet opposition to specific protection or allocation decisions.[19]

Another important issue raised at the outset of our discussion was the stability of the economic policy-making process. With the exception of the phase in which direct foreign investment was welcomed, the major themes in Brazilian economic policy remained reasonably stable throughout these years. This continuity held despite changes and serious tensions in other areas of Brazilian politics. In the period 1947–1964, there were three presidential elections, two *coups d'etat*, and perhaps most important, considerable day-to-day tensions with rumors of coup and countercoup.

In discussing politics in Brazil, perhaps more than in other less-developed countries, however, we should be aware of the different "arenas"—the diverse political structures conditioning the

[19] If corruption is much less important in influencing Brazilian policy-making than is often alleged, the question arises as to why Brazilians have given it so much importance in their discussions. Some material on this subject, emphasizing the importance of certain themes in Brazilian political culture, is presented in Chapter 7.

resolution of issues in different areas.[20] In addition to economic policy, there is the arena for foreign policy; for constitutional questions (in the sense of legitimacy, the basic distribution of power, and the rules of the political contest), in which the military have been prominent; and the "prestige arena," in which the professional politicians compete for status and position. It was a central feature of economic policy-making in the postwar period that until 1963–1964, economic policy issues were not involved in the constitutional arena. At the same time, much of the maneuvering in Brazilian politics was in the prestige arena, and instability there did not affect national economic policy-making. When presidents have been deposed in Brazil, it was because of tensions in the other arenas; and, in fact, the main economic policies—promotion of import-substituting industrialization, development of economic infrastructure, and the expanded public-sector economic role—were maintained with remarkable stability.[21]

This stability was related to the fact that the main economic policy problems with which the government had to deal as well as the ideological framework within which they were interpreted remained relatively constant throughout the period. In particular, the continuing balance-of-payments problem both oriented the government toward certain decisions, and limited the range of policy options among which it could choose. Instruction 70 is a good example of the stability induced by this constraint. According to political insiders, the Finance Minister was personally against "overly hasty" industrialization, which he blamed for the country's inflation and for the problems engendered by rapid urbanization; and the Instruction was part of a broad stabilization program which included a 38 percent devaluation. The measure was indeed hailed by the coffee planters as a blow to import substitution and a "New Deal" in Brazilian economic policy.[22]

[20] For a discussion of the concept of different political "arenas," see T. J. Lowi, "American Business, Public Policy, Case-Studies, and Political Theory," *World Politics* (July 1964).

[21] This has also been noted by other observers. Cf. the following statement from "Fifteen Years of Economic Policy in Brazil," *Economic Bulletin for Latin America* (November 1964), p. 205: "In the past, Brazil has shown a remarkable capacity for insulating infrastructure programmes from the vicissitudes of political life."

[22] Something of the feelings of the Minister, Osvaldo Aranha, appears in his statement of purpose at the time: "To restrict prudently the speed of the process of industrialization" [Augusto de Bulhões, *Os Ministros da*

Nevertheless, since discrimination against exports continued, and exchange depreciation operated more on the import exchange rate than on the export rate, even devaluation did not greatly improve the balance of payments.[23] Consequently, restrictions on imports continued, and, against the intentions of its principal authors, the Instruction came to constitute an important support for Brazilian industrialization.

This episode also illustrates the operation of the other great constant of the policy-making process—the approach of the decision-makers. No one except the traditional export sector and the international agencies, both of whom were discredited for elite opinion, proposed an alternative to import substitution and industrialization for dealing with the country's economic problems. Because of the relative stability in the policy-makers' interpretation of the country's problems,—shifts in influential opinion occurred over several years, permitting policy to adjust gradually, rather than with sharp zigzags—the tensions in other areas of Brazilian politics did not greatly affect economic policy-making. Furthermore, to ensure *administrative* stability, most public-sector economic activities have been carried on through autonomous corporations with their own operating income, or through agencies with specially earmarked tax revenues.[24] This has given them an important measure of budgetary autonomy and insulation against political shifts.

The major exceptions to economic-policy stability were the

Fazenda (Rio de Janeiro, 1956), p. 223]. Close associates of Aranha and Getúlio testify that they were taken aback by the problems created by urbanization and inflation and that industrialization also went against their agrarian ideals.

On the expectations of the planters, see the speeches of Salvio de Almeida, spokesman of the coffee planters' association, in *Dez Anos na Política do Café* (São Paulo, 1956).

[23] As mentioned earlier, after the 1953 devaluation brought about under Instruction 70, a considerable spread was maintained between the import and the export exchange rates, the latter going to the government as an export tax. In addition to exchange overvaluation, quotas and export prohibitions continued to penalize exports of primary products other than coffee.

[24] A partial list of government corporations and activities with earmarked taxes or budget revenues includes the National Development Bank, coffee retention, electricity, railways, road construction, ship-building, and the Development Authorities for the Northeast, Southwest, and Amazon regions.

periodic episodes of monetary stabilization. With the continuing inflation and balance-of-payments deficit, every few years brought an effort at stabilization. This was usually required by Brazil's international creditors and was sometimes also supported, for a time, by elite opinion, in reaction against the heightened inflation and the "corruption" that had accompanied the prior spurts of public-sector expansion and economic growth. Such periods of moral and fiscal austerity occurred in 1952–1953, in 1955, in 1958–1959, and in 1961.

These stabilization phases were in a sense Brazil's version of the business cycle in traditional capitalist economies. The ceiling on output was determined by the availability of foreign credits for imports in the worsening balance-of-payments situation and heightened inflation that preceded each stabilization episode.[25] These periodic incidents usually entailed an exchange-rate depreciation and attempts to reduce the government deficit by cutting public-sector expenditure.

Devaluation, however, only reinforced the trend toward import substitution, while the impact of the restrictive monetary and fiscal measures was greatly limited by the factors discussed above, which gave continuity to economic policy formation. In particular, the political elite's commitment to economic development ended the monetary stabilization programs as soon as they appeared seriously to restrict economic growth; [26] and the autonomy of most public-sector investment programs prevented major changes in government economic activity.

[25] The sequence usually went from inflation (in part for the reasons discussed in Chapter 9), to a deteriorating balance-of-payments situation and import supply which was increasingly inelastic with respect to domestic income and production, to accelerated inflation. Since the dampening effect came directly from the need to meet or anticipate the terms of foreign lenders such as the International Monetary Fund, however, the cycle has appeared to be the exclusive result of policy action and political factors. Because of its prominence in these episodes, the IMF has been the focus for hostility which would have no such immediate and personal target in systems where disinflation proceeds, perhaps much more painfully, through impersonal market forces or the operation of the international gold standard.

[26] Perhaps because of its diplomatic leverage or its skill in handling the international agencies, until 1963 Brazil was always able to secure additional foreign credits without going very far in the stabilization program. Further discussion of the politics of stabilization appears in Chapter 9.

As Table 17 indicates, although there were some fluctuations, in no year did public-sector expenditure actually decline. At the most, austerity-minded finance ministers were able to cut mar-

TABLE 17. *Growth of Real Public Sector Expenditure, 1948–1960*

Year	Annual Increase
1948	13%
1949	9
1950	4
1951	13
1952	2
1953	14
1954	12
1955	0
1956	20
1957	16
1958	11
1959	9
1960	11

Source. Computed from material supplied by Fundação Getúlio Vargas

ginal investments, without greatly reducing the aggregate of government spending. Hence even the stabilization efforts did not greatly interrupt the course of economic policy-making; but they appeared only as cycles in the strong secular trend of expanding public-sector economic activity.

Finally, we should note one other key feature of Brazilian economic policy-making. Because of conditions we will discuss below, almost all of the major decisions that shaped the course of postwar Brazilian growth—the de facto rejection of export expansion, the emphasis on investment programs in infrastructure and "basic industries," the public-sector expenditure that led to the large government deficits and the increases in aggregate demand—were made in an atmosphere singularly free of political activity and conflict.[27] Indeed, these decisions were hardly

[27] The only exceptions were the controversies concerning the government oil company and the policy concerning direct foreign investment. Regard-

"made" in a conscious sense, so much as walked into, with little perception of practical alternatives. Policy decisions were politicized only at the stage when details which did not affect the main lines of the policy were reached.[28] In Part II we will discuss the conditions which led to this situation. Before proceeding to that discussion, however, let us consider some of the conditions underlying Brazilian economic policy-making.

Some Underlying Conditions

In principle, economic policy-making has a potential for arousing enormous conflict in determining how the gains and costs of alternative policies will be distributed among different groups in society. Conditions that modulate or intensify this conflict are especially important in transitional societies, where, it is sometimes suggested, the political order may be too fragile to withstand overly violent conflict. Alternatively, extensive struggle may lead to immobilism in policy-making, and the country's economic growth suffers because important policy issues cannot be resolved. Fortunately for Brazil, certain underlying conditions have mitigated the conflict surrounding economic policy formulation, and reduced problems of either stalemate or shattering division.

HISTORICAL CONDITIONS OF BRAZILIAN DEVELOPMENT

First, the special historical conditions of Brazilian development softened some of the basic conflicts associated with industrialization in other countries. As noted in Chapter 2, tariffs on manufactured products and protection against agricultural imports were established *together*. The export interests and the in-

___

less of the passions they aroused, neither of these decisions had a major impact on the course of macroeconomic growth.
[28] For example, a major feature of government allocation policy was the strong public-sector support for steel production. Here it was taken for granted that steel had to be supplied from domestic manufacture rather than from foreign trade. Because of the magnitude of the capital commitment involved, there was also no debate on the issue of a direct public-sector economic role. It was only after these major decisions had been taken that political activity began, as, for example, regional interests contested the location of the steel mill for São Paulo, Minas Gerais, or Rio de Janeiro.

dustrialists also shared an important policy goal in undervaluation of the exchange rate.

Furthermore, conflict between the government and the industrialists and opposition to a strong economic role for the public sector, characteristic in the United States, for example, have also been relatively minor. In Brazil, a strong government power antedated the emergence of the manufacturing interests, and they were never strong enough to expect political dominance. On the contrary, the government appeared as the potential patron of the emerging industrial class, providing them with tariff protection and other policy support. And looking from the other direction, the intelligentsia and the political elite have generally avoided attacking the industrialists, whom they have seen as Schumpeterian entrepreneurs promoting national development rather than Marxian capitalists drinking the blood of the poor.[29]

The government's political dominance also mitigated conflict between capital and labor. The major issue under contention has been wages. However, led by the government, the industrialists have been amenable to periodic rises in the minimum wage, since the government permitted them to adjust with price increases. Such harmony did not always exist. From accounts of the São Paulo industrialists in the 1920's and 1930's—with their extensive strike-breaking activities and opposition to trade unions and higher wages—it appears that only the political support of Getúlio Vargas for urban labor induced the industrialists to take the nonantagonistic approach.[30] Partly because of government wage policy, the industrial work-force has been recruited at wage rates far above those of agricultural workers. Under the conditions of buoyant demand and accelerated industrialization, both the industrialists and the factory workers have seen themselves as part of the same expanding modern sector. Thus, while Getúlio Vargas

[29] Since the early 1960's, this view of the national industrialists may have changed. See, for example, Hélio Jaguaribe's condemnation of the "consular bourgeoisie"—a concept very similar to Paul Baran's "compradores"—in his essay, "The Dynamics of Brazilian Nationalism," in Claudio Veliz (ed.), *Obstacles to Change in Latin America*, (London, 1965), esp. pp. 182–187. Characteristically, the industrialists are not condemned for exploiting the Brazilian workers but are taken to task for collaborating with foreign interests.

[30] See Warren Dean, "São Paulo's Industrial Elite, 1890–1960" (Ph.D. dissertation, University of Florida, 1964), pp. 94–115.

could be hailed by the urban lower classes as the "Father of the Poor," the upper classes could add, "and the Mother of the Rich." Consequently, the classic pattern of nineteenth-century European industrialization, involving violent conflict between labor and capital, was largely avoided.

Brazil's rapid economic growth, at rates twice as high as those of Europe or the United States in their periods of industrialization, was another basic factor conditioning politics during this period. Economic development in itself ultimately lost some of its appeal to the intelligentsia and elite opinion, but growing per capita income probably satisfied aspirations and reduced the strains placed on the political system. All groups—even rural workers [31]—saw their real income rise during this period, and none had to sacrifice from his absolute income level to finance the benefits of others. Differential gains from development occurred only at the margin, where they probably did not arouse as much reaction as absolute reductions.

The potential conflict associated with economic development was also mitigated by the political genius of Getúlio Vargas, the politician who presided over much of this process. Quite apart from any charismatic qualities, he had the political skills of temporization, dissembling, concilation, and ruthlessness necessary to reduce debilitating conflict among different groups within the modern sector, while avoiding a continuing frontal collision with traditional groups. As noted in Chapter 2, during his first administration, from 1931 to 1945, Getúlio was relatively uninterested in industrialization, and he contributed little in the way of policy directly promoting economic development. But his political skills helped the country over the period of political transition and reduced the political strains accompanying economic change.

THE BALANCE-OF-PAYMENTS PROBLEM

Finally, we should note the importance of the balance-of-payments problem as a basic feature of the framework within which economic policy issues were approached during this period. Because of its international implications, this problem took

[31] *Plano Trienal de Desenvolvimento Econômico e Social* (written under the direction of Celso Furtado), (Rio de Janeiro, 1962), pp. 26–27.

overriding priority as an issue which the policy-makers could not avoid. As a result, the payments crisis served to orient the government in its selection and treatment of policy issues. Moreover, because of this problem's wide-ranging implications—for protection and resource allocation—the government's tasks were structured in many areas. The chronic payments imbalance likewise served to narrow the area of possible choice in decision-making.[32] Thus it reduced political conflict in the formulation of economic policy. Perhaps most important, the balance-of-payments problem influenced the way in which many of Brazil's economic problems were formulated politically. Because of its primacy as a national problem, many issues of economic policy were approached as involving the country *as a whole*, not as issues in which different socioeconomic groups had different interests. Foreign-exchange shortage also evoked a crisis atmosphere that contributed to the acceptance of many decisions purporting to deal with it.

In orienting policy and reducing choice and conflict, the balance-of-payments problem played a role similar to the Cold War in the politics of American defense policy during the postwar period. Once the situation was perceived as a threat to basic security, certain policy actions *had* to be taken. At the same time, the range of possible options and the scope for domestic conflict on foreign policy issues were greatly reduced. Finally, here too, a crisis atmosphere and the issue of the national interest—with the nation considered as an organic whole—have been evoked, reducing potential conflict in an atmosphere of bipartisanship.

[32] The constraint which foreign-exchange shortage imposed on the range of policy options open to Brazil in many areas applied only in the short-run. Because of the persistence of the doctrines within which the problem was approached, however, the short-run became the long-run.

Part II

Politics and Economic Policy in Postwar Brazil

CHAPTER 7

The Influence of Industry and the Autonomy of Government

In Part I the general picture that emerged was one in which the government, largely the Presidency, acted with considerable political autonomy in formulating and carrying out economic policy decisions. Even the influence of the industrialists, one of the strongest potential contenders, appears to have been either marginal or limited to issues on which the government had no firm views of its own.[1]

Presidential elections offer another example of the industrialists' relatively weak political position. Despite the enormous importance of the chief executive, the industrialists play almost no role in the process of selecting candidates. Presidential nominees are chosen by the professional politicians of the leading political cliques, and it is almost unthinkable that a particular candidate would have to be acceptable to the Confederation of Industries or even the broader group of "industry." Individual industrialists may participate in the nominating process either directly, as part of the entourage of contending individuals, or through professional politicians with whom they have arrangements. As we shall see, however, such a pattern of individual political action substantially weakens the political voice of the industrialist group as a whole. The Confederation of Industries simply lacks the

[1] Some other observers have also reached similar conclusions concerning Brazilian economic policymaking. For example, a prominent Brazilian political sociologist, Fernando Henrique Cardoso, in his *Empresário Industrial e Desenvolvimento Econômico no Brasil* (São Paulo, 1964), esp. pp. 159–187, also interprets the industrialists as political dependents of the state, a system he describes as "sub-capitalism." Cf. also the references to Francisco Weffort, as cited below.

power to take a decisive role in the nominating or electoral process. Hence it adopts the strategy of waiting until the outcome is decided, and then attempts to reach an accommodation with the victor. This reactive attitude does not constitute a basis for subsequent strong interventions.

There is no evidence that the President's freedom from party or interest-group pressures lessened in the early 1960's. After the election of Jânio Quadros, for example:

> *For several months, no one knew or would publicly venture a firm prediction about any important policy decision or appointment that the new President would make.* The suspense was genuine—the parties, the press, and the private citizen give themselves entirely to what was openly acknowledged to be a guessing game. The *União Democrática Nacional,* the party that had made Quadros its candidate, was as much perplexed in victory about its future as were its rivals in defeat.[2]

This picture does not suggest a President bound by commitments to political parties and interest groups which pose serious constraints on his autonomy.

Our suggestion that industrial interests have not had the power to act as strong independent participants in the economic policy-making process differs, however, from some interpretations, which have seen the industrialists as "the sector which in practice formulated economic policy in Brazil."[3] Let us therefore attempt to substantiate this view of Brazilian politics by considering how industrialist interest articulation has functioned, and what may be the causes of a relatively weak political position.

Techniques of Interest Articulation

Industrial interests have had several ways of pressing their views on the government. The oldest and most traditional is through representation by Congressmen speaking for their interests. Such representatives provide information to the government concerning their clients' preferences and may represent them as negotia-

---

[2] Frank Bonilla, "A National Ideology for Development: Brazil," in Kalman H. Silvert (ed.), *Expectant Peoples: Nationalism and Development* (New York, 1963), pp. 254–255. The italics are Bonilla's.
[3] "Fifteen Years of Economic Policy in Brazil," *Economic Bulletin for Latin America* (November 1964), p. 190.

tors on specific issues. As soon as we mention this mode of interest articulation, however, one important feature immediately
shows itself—the fragmentation of industrialist interest articulation. Whereas some Congressmen speak for the Confederation of
Industries or individual trade associations, many others speak for
individual businessmen or cliques who constitute part of their
political clientele.

Such political representatives have their base in the legislature,
which they use both for participation on the committees special-
izing in economic policy and as a sounding board for access to
elite opinion. As Brazilian political power has become increasingly concentrated in the Presidency and in the government
ministries, however, interest articulation has also shifted its locus.

A major activity of interest representatives has been the
maintenance of contacts and communication with officials in the
key economic agencies such as the Finance Ministry, the Monetary Authority, the Development Bank, and the import and
credit departments of the *Banco do Brasil*. These agencies, however, have been politically protected by the President from direct
pressure by interest groups. Their senior personnel, who make
the important decisions, generally also have a clean reputation
concerning graft. And as we will see in Chapter 8, the high economic administrators have been members of a cadre of career
civil servants who are not easily open to close ties with, or more
subtle influence from, private interests.[4]

In these conditions, the interest groups' principal mode of influencing the *técnicos* has been by provision of economic data
and analysis. For this purpose, the industrialist interest groups
have maintained extensive technical staffs. In the general pattern
of such interest articulation, the business groups have reacted to a
policy orientation already decided, and have provided information to convince the government that its aims could better be

[4] These considerations apply only to the key economic agencies cited,
which determined the main lines of allocation and foreign trade policy.
Some of the sectoral agencies, notably in coffee and sugar, are reputed to
have been taken over politically by the interests they were supposed to
regulate. But as noted in Chapter 2 (pp. 20–25, and on sugar, n. 46 there)
such "colonization" did not prevent the major economic policy decisions
in these areas from being taken directly against the interests of these
private groups.

served by modifications suggested by the industrialists. In the give-and-take of such contacts there has clearly been scope for changing the government's original policy, but the industrialists' activity has largely been limited within the framework established by the government.

Another important technique of industrialist interest articulation has been by means of public relations activity such as press campaigns. For example, at the instigation of the domestic copper-refining interests, newspaper articles may appear to applaud the industry's technical achievements and warn of the threat that copper imports pose to the development of so "basic" a national industry. In adopting this instrument the industrialist groups have recognized that their ability to *command* the government by threatening political sanctions is relatively limited and that their best chance for success is to influence the political elite through a channel to which they are more susceptible—"public opinion." This technique has also attempted to overcome one of the major political liabilities under which business interests have labored: namely, that their claims are "egoistic" and concerned only with their own "selfish" interests. By such public relations activity, the industrialists attempt to associate their position with the ideology of national development and try to show a coincidence between their interests and those of the country as a whole.

Although industrialist interest groups do not have a very strong power position vis-à-vis the government, they do perform a "capillary" function in building consensus and in transmitting information between businessmen and the government. This activity is particularly important because, due to lack of channels of communication, there is a great deal of mutual ignorance. The government may not be well-informed about conditions in industry, and the industrialists may have little idea about the government's goals. Consequently, transmission of information, with the Confederation of Industries and other trade associations taking the role of intermediary, provides a basis for more rational action on both sides.

Let us now consider why the industrialists have not had the power to play the role of a strong, independent bargainer in Brazilian policy-making.

Causes of the Political Weakness of Industrial Interests

First, we should emphasize that because of certain themes in Brazilian political culture *all* pressure groups are placed at a disadvantage. From interviews with government officials, interest groups, and industrialists, it appears that, with a strong Rousseauean flavor, Brazilian political culture takes an organic view of society and politics, and believes in policies framed for the "general interest" of the nation considered as a whole.[5] Nationalism as a pervasive ideology leads strongly in this direction because of its focus on the body politic as an organic whole.[6] And it would not be a great exaggeration to say that, in line with this approach, efforts by private interests to influence public policy are considered *inherently* "corrupt." By the same token, government action which is fashioned in deference to particular claims and pressures from society is considered "demagogy." This political philosophy differs sharply, of course, from the doctrine in the United States, which considers that the public interest is well-served by the participation of private groups, and that the influence of private groups on government decision-making is the essence of democracy.

Within the Brazilian framework, however, the claims of interest groups have little legitimacy, for they are distrusted as selfish and are discounted heavily because of their obvious "egoism." In a system of elite politics where prestige and moral authority count for a great deal, therefore, "special" interests are at a severe disadvantage. Furthermore, because of the structural features (discussed below) which have weakened interest groups in Brazil, such normative conceptions in the political culture can in fact take effect; and Brazilian governments have been able to avoid granting private groups an important participant role in the policy-making process.

The political disadvantages of the special group can, to a

[5] These themes are closely related to the "nonantagonistic" framework within which, as Albert Hirschman and others have noted, economic policy issues have often been approached in Brazil.
[6] The frequent emphasis in Brazil on the need for a *tomada de consciência*, a moral consultation of the people's will to deal with national problems, is directly out of Rousseau.

limited extent, be overcome by appropriating labels of the general interest. For example, the labor unions have had their moral and political position greatly strengthened by appearing as the spokesmen of "the People" (*O Povo*). The industrialists have also attempted to gain greater legitimacy by claiming the appellation of "the Productive Classes" and speaking in the name of "industrialization" and "development." Interviews with both industrialist spokesmen and their political targets among the administrators, however, indicate that such claims are not pressed with any self-assurance and are received very skeptically. The industrialists have never been able unabashedly to take the position that what was best for themselves was best for the country as a whole. Hence, even when speaking in terms of broad national interests, industrial spokesmen have lacked the moral stature, both in their own eyes and in those of other political participants, to claim the deference that might be theirs in systems that give more respect to private interests.

These disadvantages are increased by the allocation of roles in Brazilian political culture. Government and trade association officials alike indicate that in their view only the government is charged with responsibility for the needs of the entire nation. Hence the industrialists have been considered trespassers—and probably with dubious motives—when they have attempted to enter broader spheres of policy-making. Moreover, Brazilian industrialists have not had an independent view of their own for dealing with national problems.[7] When they have presented policy initiatives, they have been effectively countered for not taking into account broader national requirements. As a result, they have been forced into a defensive posture, reacting to initiatives formulated by the government.[8]

Brazil's industrialists have also been hampered by certain conditions stemming from the historical pattern of the country's

[7] In the United States, this function has been filled by the ideology discussed by S. E. Harris et al., *The American Business Creed* (Cambridge, Mass., 1956).

[8] Fernando Henrique Cardoso, *op. cit.*, p. 175, has also emphasized the essentially reactive posture of Brazilian industrialists in their political activity. In an effort to reduce their tactical disability, a new industrialist organization, the National Planning Association (ANPES), was established in early 1964, to provide general perspective and high-level policy analysis of the sort prepared by the institution of the same name in the United States.

industrialization. For one thing, they have not enjoyed the same political alliances with other business and propertied interests which have supported manufacturing interests in many advanced countries. Historically, Brazilian industry emerged in a context of conflict with other business interests, particularly the commercial groups associated with the import trade, who, indeed, were the industrialists' chief political opponents. By way of compensation, the industrialists have had as political allies the urban middle strata and the intelligentsia, who have stood with them on most questions affecting government support for industry. The absence of a generalized alliance with other propertied interests, however, has meant that in the Congress the industrialists have not had sufficient votes to take a commanding posture. Moreover, since Brazilian industrialization has been concentrated in only a few states, whereas national politics are organized on a federal basis, the nonindustrial states have been able to exercise disproportionate influence at the national level. As a result, the industrialists have often been in the position of a minority petitioning the government rather than a group with a sufficient political support to impose its wishes.

Reacting to this situation, industrialist groups initiated some new political activities in the early 1960's. One organization established was the *IBAD* (Brazilian Institute for Democratic Action), which attempted to control a greater number of congressional votes. Another new effort was the *IPES* (Institute for Economic and Social Research), which attempted to exercise a strong and systematic influence, speaking for the industrialists as a whole, in the communications media. It is still too early to appraise the effects of these initiatives, but their impact may well be limited because of other conditions that have hampered Brazilian industrialists in their political activity.

Even less than in many advanced countries, Brazil's industrialists do not constitute a homogeneous group acting together with a unity of political purpose. Apart from the usual regional differences and conflicts between different industries, the social origins and composition of Brazilian industrialists are very heterogeneous.[9] Descendants of immigrants from a variety of countries

[9] In this paragraph, I follow closely upon Cardoso, pp. 160–164. His work was based on an interview and questionnaire study of Brazilian industrialists.

and native Brazilians of very diverse socioeconomic backgrounds, the industrialists do not share a common tradition. The dynamic pace of industrialization has also added to their ranks so rapidly that some industrialists have not developed a strong class consciousness in their new situation. As a result, Brazilian industrialists have not allowed themselves to be mobilized to the full extent of their "objective" political potential. Indeed, instead of acting together under the leadership of the Confederation of Industries, individual industrialists and rival "groups" usually compete with each other for political access. Their competition is all the more fierce because the political role allocated to the class as a whole is limited.

Following this pattern of individual self-interest rather than cohesive class action, betrayals by trade association leaders have also been important. The government has used graft to control trade association leaders; for example, industrialist spokesmen have accepted loans from the *Banco do Brasil* for their firms and given up their associations' broader claims. Such "sellouts" have been an important factor in reducing class and trade association pressure on the government. And by bringing the taint of corruption into the interest group itself, they have reduced still further the participation and support of individual industrialists.

Not only has lack of class consciousness hindered the industrialists, but their relatively recent arrival on the Brazilian scene, after the professional politicians and the bureaucracy, has also been a serious handicap. As in some other societies such as Italy and Spain, in which industrialization came relatively late, the state penetrated and took control of the interest groups rather than let them develop as an independent power center. This occurred openly during the Vargas "corporatist" dictatorship of 1937–1945, when class associations were directly controlled by the government. It has continued to recent years, as the Confederation of Industries' income comes from a tax levied and administered by the government. Through its control over these resources, the government has been able to restrict the Confederation's autonomy, for example, in selection of its leaders. This phenomenon of *peleguismo*—the President's nomination of interest-group leaders—has been especially marked with the labor unions, but it has also occurred with the business associations.[10]

Finally, reinforcing its dominance, the government has available policy instruments which give it decisive power over the fate of many industrial enterprises. Aside from the "commanding heights" of import and credit allocation, the Brazilian government also either produces directly or regulates prices or output in most key sectors.[11] It has been able to use these economic powers either to win over or to coerce trade association leaders or individual industrialists, thus splitting and weakening the class as a whole. As this suggests, it would be misleading to interpret the industrialists' political weakness as a lack of correspondence of political power with economic position.[12] On the contrary, the government's ability to dominate private interests is partly due to *its* command over the material resources of society. Economic development has brought a rapid expansion of the private manufacturing sector, but the growth of the public sector has been even more marked. Apart from the government's sheer quantitative importance in the economy, it has the two strategic vantage points just cited—discretionary control over credits and imports, both of complementary inputs and of competitive products. Through the National Development Bank and the *Banco do Brasil*, the government determines the allocation of short- and long-term investment funds, and has all the power, subtle and crude, which in capitalist countries is often attributed to "Wall Street." [13]

[10] Cf. Francisco Weffort, "Estado y Masas en el Brasil," *Revista Latino-americana de Sociología*, **65** (1), p. 60: "In effect, all the important organizations which present themselves as intermediaries between the State and individuals are really better understood as parts of the State itself, rather than genuinely autonomous bodies."

This may be one of the significant differences between Brazilian and Argentine politics. In Argentina functional groups appear as more genuinely autonomous bodies with their own power base. Another important difference is Brazilian political culture's Rousseauean emphasis, noted previously, on policy solutions framed for the nation as a whole. This is very different from the "anti-nationalist" attitude described by Kalman Silvert in his discussion of Argentina in *Expectant Peoples*.

[11] For a list of the Brazilian government's production and regulatory activities, see "Fifteen Years of Economic Policy in Brazil," pp. 196–197.

[12] Kalman Silvert and Frank Bonilla, "Education and the Social Meaning of Development" (mimeo, 1963), pp. 8–11.

[13] Just the threat of calling in loans outstanding to the *Banco do Brasil* has been enough to reduce even the largest private economic groups to sub-

The government's ability to use its economic policy instruments to manipulate the interest groups reflects the strong position it has developed both because of historical reasons and more recently because of the major structural feature of Brazilian politics—the system of clientelistic politics.

Clientelistic Politics and the Autonomy of Government

Brazilian politics have often been described as "clientelistic" or patronage politics.[14] That is, Congressmen and other politicians are elected and maintain themselves in office largely on the basis of the patronage they trade for the electoral support of individuals and groups within their district. In this pattern, politicians organize individual political machines which mobilize financial support, public relations, and voters. This support may be drawn from a variety of sources—individuals, cliques, family, and business associates, local newspapers, individual firms, and previously organized political groupings such as clubs, trade associations, and trade unions. Some public-sector economic corporations have also been important sources of financial and organizational support for politicians. In return, the politician provides political representation for his clients vis-à-vis the government, especially in matters of loans, imports, and tax treatment.

Such machines of individual politicians begin at the local (município) level and, with arrangements among other politicians, may extend over broader areas. In cases such as Adhemar de Barros in São Paulo, the political organization may extend over an entire state. Taking on some general ideological or programmatic coloring, it may even become a "political party." The center of the machine, however, is the political career of the

mission. Brazil's persistent inflation has strengthened the government's hand in dealing with the industrialists because the inflation has eroded the real value of their working capital. Hence businessmen have constantly been placed in the position of petitioners for additional short-term credit— merely to maintain their existing market position.

[14] For a discussion of clientelistic politics in Brazil, see Hélio Jaguaribe, *O Nacionalismo na Atualidade Brasileira* (Rio de Janeiro, 1958), pp. 40 ff., and in a more recent statement, "As Eleições de '62," *Tempo Brasileiro.* Jaguaribe places much more emphasis on the importance of government jobs as the principal payoff in the system, as opposed to the other material incentives which I have stressed. His interpretation of the effects of the system is also different from the one suggested below.

politician who controls it, and the favors he can supply to his clients. We should also emphasize that clientelistic politics is neither "old style" nor necessarily rural. This pattern of politics may have had its origin in the older rural-dominated society; but one of the key features of modern Brazilian politics is the extent to which politicians entering the system have also functioned in this manner, including those based in urban and industrial areas.

Such clientelistic politics appear very similar to the classical model of political machines in American cities. Banfield and Wilson give the following description of this sort of political system, in terms very close to those used by Jaguaribe and other authors to describe Brazilian clientelistic politics:

> A political "machine" is a party organization that depends crucially upon inducements that are both *specific* and *material*. . . . The machine, therefore, is apolitical: it is interested only in making and distributing income . . . to those who run it and work for it. Political principle is foreign to it.[15]

The inherent lack of political principle, and the importance of inducements that are "specific" and "material," as opposed to general and ideological, have given clientelistic politics a bad name among most Brazilian intellectuals. I shall suggest below, however, that coming together with other features of Brazilian politics, this system has made possible both the centralization of power and the opportunity for ideologically oriented policy-making that many Brazilians also prefer.[16]

[15] Edwin C. Banfield and James Q. Wilson, *City Politics* (Cambridge, Mass., 1965), pp. 115–116. See also Martin Meyerson and Edwin C. Banfield, *Politics, Planning, and the Public Interest* (Glencoe, Ill., 1955), the chapter on "The Politicians."

[16] The failure to take account of possible beneficial effects of clientelist politics may have occurred because the system goes strongly against the ideological goal of democracy: machine politics are not supposed to be true democracy. This attitude was also characteristic of early American approaches to this question, but for revisionist views, see V. O. Key, *The Techniques of Political Graft in the United States* (privately printed, 1936); Robert K. Merton, *Social Theory and Social Structure* (New York, 1959), pp. 19–85; Harold Lasswell, "Bribery," in *The Encyclopedia of the Social Sciences* (New York, 1930), Vol. II. For a classic statement of the centralizing effects of political machines, which permits effective formulation and execution of policy in a system in which power would otherwise be widely dispersed, see Henry Jones Ford, "Municipal Reform," *Political Science Quarterly*, No. 4 (1904).

Clientelistic Politics versus Group Politics

Although clientelistic politics and class or interest-group politics may sometimes overlap, the stress of many observers on clientelistic politics in Brazil suggests that this is the modal pattern giving the political system its distinctive structure. Let us therefore consider the implications of such a system for national economic policy-making. We can approach this question by highlighting some of the important differences between clientelistic politics and the more familiar models of class and interest-group politics.[17]

First, the goals of the political actors are likely to differ. In a system of class or group politics the primary aim of the contending parties is to implement their orientations and interests into general policy. By contrast, in clientelistic politics the politicians generally approach the government with requests for specific favors to accommodate their client. Whereas class politics focuses on the creation of broad policy, with programs and perspectives seen in general terms, clientelistic politics aims at limited, individual modifications of established policy. For example, in a system of group politics, politicians may formulate a general allocation policy, with each group attempting to use the machinery of the state for its own benefit. Clientelistic politicians, however, concentrate rather on attaining individual government loans for their particular clients—within the framework of an already determined budget and allocational criteria.[18]

The focus on specific, material claims derives from the type of pressures operating on the politicians themselves. The major input into such a system is specific requests of individual clients, supported by direct personal rewards for the politicians, rather

[17] Despite important differences between them, interest-group and class politics share common divergences from clientelistic politics. In the present context, we shall focus on the differences between these two types of politics on the one hand and clientelistic politics on the other.

[18] Cf. Meyerson and Banfield, *loc. cit.* They also note that demands made through the intermediary of the machine involved only relatively small, specific adjustments to policies which had already been decided, and that "curiously," "nothing big" was ever asked of the bureaucratic agency they studied.

than general ideological or programmatic formulations backed by the support of broad groups. Moreover, the individual politicians have only their own individual limited perspectives; and indeed no initiative for general policy formulation may emerge from the welter of particular claims. Other institutions within the system may direct attention to general programs and issues, but effective interest aggregation is hampered by another feature of clientelistic politics—the political fragmentation of interest groups and socioeconomic classes (discussed later). In such a system, the politicians can concentrate on procuring for their clients the favors necessary for their individual political organizations. As long as enough clients are satisfied to permit election, the politicians can take as their principal goal the cultivation of their individual careers and prestige.

Another important difference between clientelistic and group politics lies in the politicians' relation to different channels of communication. In a system of group politics, politicians receive communications, both of technical data and of ideological perspective, from the interest group or socioeconomic class for whom they speak. Such messages come to the politician because he is himself very much part of the group for which he speaks—as when a businessman serves as legislator—or because they are provided by the group he represents. Clientelistic politicians, on the other hand, are not necessarily "plugged in" so directly to any such independent communications network. Hence they operate with less of the particular perspective and technical knowledge of the various groups affected by policy. In the words of Brazilian interest groups which have tried with little success to influence these politicians: "They don't know anything about coffee"; or, "They don't understand the problems of industry." And, in the absence of orienting views and data from broader social groups, the politicians are much more open to influence by the messages from within the political class itself—the elite opinion discussed in the next chapter.

A final important difference between clientelistic and group politics relates to the locus of power. In comparison with a politician elected by a group which controls his political future, a politician with a machine of his own has considerably more freedom of action. Although he may enter into *quid pro quo* arrangements with various groups, he does so at his own discretion. Precisely in order to retain his autonomy, he is likely to seek arrangements among many different groups and among individual members of various groups. As a result, interest groups and socioeconomic classes within society may be too fragmented to act cohesively.[19] Although such groups exist "objectively," their members act politically not in their group roles but as clients of individual politicians. Not only is their support denied to the interest group or class to whose strength they might have contributed, but by adhering to a different political configuration—the machine— they create a powerful political actor competing with the interest and class groups that do exist. As a result, the ability of "objective" groups to act as independent political forces and constrain the politicians is greatly reduced.

Moreover, since most political machines cross-cut many different groups in constituting their political backing, the politicians may be able to play off one client against others, rather than

[19] V. O. Key, *Southern Politics* (New York, 1950), p. 47, reaches a similar conclusion in his analysis of a system which was not too different: "Personalization of leadership fractionalizes the electorate." Although Key states this in terms of personalistic leadership, most of his analysis through the study runs in terms of political machines and clientelistic politics. Although flamboyant and attractive personalities may help mobilize voter support, patronage is the essence of the system he describes and leads, as he emphasizes throughout the book, to relatively weak interest groups and class pressures.

We should note the relevance of this study by Key, researched in the southern states in the late 1940's, for analysis of political development. Key was concerned with politics in the conditions of sharply restricted electorate and weak interest group or party structures, and hence the absence of programmatic or ideological politics that could cope with the region's economic problems (pp. 307 ff.). Many of the features he notes are relevant for Latin American politics; for example, politics in some states is limited to the local notables (pp. 187 ff.); the political impact of the return of the GI veterans, who had, however, no clear ideological goals other than "clean elections" (pp. 204 ff.); the alliance of outside capitalists, largely in primary products, with local politicians. His discussion of Huey Long's "populist politics" (pp. 156–183) is strikingly reminiscent of Getúlio Vargas. As suggested further in our analysis, however, Key's conclusion, that such a political structure is inherently unable to cope with economic problems, does not necessarily follow. If, as in Brazil during this period, the political elite was primarily concerned with economic development rather than, as in the South, holding down the Negroes, then the same political system could produce very different economic policy results.

be placed in the situation of captive to specific supporters.[20] Hence, in far greater measure, the politicians are able to form an independent political elite, without the restraining power of political forces outside of the professional political class. Insulated from pressures coming from the broader society, they can act with a fair measure of autonomy.[21]

Clientelistic Politics in Brazil

Such a situation of patronage and machine politics seems to have developed in Brazil, in a structure described by Banfield and Wilson as "moderate centralization in the business sphere but much centralization [through a strong political machine] in the political one." [22] In such a case, "The relatively poorly organized business leaders compete with each other by advancing mutually incompatible proposals; under the circumstances, they have little influence on [the Chief Executive]. In a particular matter (although not, perhaps in *all* matters), he can safely ignore their efforts to influence him." We see evidence of such a pattern not only in the widely noted practice of *clientelismo* but also in one of its effects: the substantial freedom of government action that we observed in the case studies of economic policy.

The conditions that weaken the power of interest groups in Brazilian politics stand out more clearly if we consider the major exceptions to the dominant pattern—regional interests and the military. There has been no lack of regional self-identification in Brazil. At the same time, the federal constitution provides a ready-made structure in which to express this political consciousness. In

[20] The fact that political machines are based on disparate sources of political support and cut across different groups may be one of the structural features associated with the much-noted ability of Brazilian politicians and Brazilian politics to reach compromise solutions in cases of apparently frontal conflict of interests.

[21] This has also been observed by other students of Brazilian politics. Cf., for example, a similar conclusion reached by Weffort, p. 57, in different terms: "We find ourselves, then, before the following situation; those with political power do not represent the groups which dominate the basic sectors of the economy. This means that the new governmental configuration has a basic difference in comparison with the former; it is no longer the immediate expression of the hierarchy of economic power."

[22] This and the following quotation are from Banfield and Wilson, p. 274.

consequence, the state governments and the regional *bancadas* (delegations) in the Congress have been among the few participants with an independent bargaining position in Brazilian politics. With their strong corporate sense, the military too have not had their political position weakened by insufficient class consciousness. They have also not suffered either because of a late arrival on the political scene or because of internal splits and adherence to different political machines.

The relatively powerful position of the military, in contrast to the industrialists, is exemplified in the way the Finance Minister, the official with principal responsibility for economic policy, is chosen. These ministers are appointed as the President's personal agents rather than as the class representatives of "industry" or the "business community." The individuals chosen have usually had experience in banking or industry, for this has been considered a prerequisite for technical competence. In political terms, appointees have been selected on the basis of an arrangement between the President and the individual businessman or his clique. But the minister has been regarded as the President's man rather than someone imposed by the business sector to deal with their affairs in government.[23] By contrast, the military as a group have been able to exercise a much greater say in choosing the administrative heads of the armed service ministries.[24] These have been regarded as, and have functioned as the representatives of the military—rather than of the President—in the government.

The military, however, are the conspicuous exception to the rule of Brazilian politics. Elsewhere the system has entailed the transfer of political power to the professional politicians. And, in what is perhaps the major theme in modern Brazilian political his-

[23] The industrialists have had a much greater voice in the choice of the Minister of Industry and Commerce. His role in economic policy-making has been relatively minor, however. For example, President Kubitschek's Development Council had 14 members (mostly cabinet members), but the Minister of Industry was not included. In 1959, membership was expanded to 18, and he was admitted. These data are from Robert Daland, *Brazilian Planning* (Chapel Hill, 1967), p. 88, n. 3.

[24] Although the President has a measure of discretion in choosing the Military Ministers, the crucial condition is that they must be acceptable to the officer corps. In cases where the President tried to overstep this condition, he was invariably forced to back down, with the resignation of his chosen Minister.

tory, this power has been concentrated in the hands of the President, with the development since the 1930's of a centralized political apparatus dominating the local and state machines. By determining the distribution of credit, imports, and tax dispensations, the President has had the carrot-and-stick power to control the lesser politicians. Good relations with the President have become a *sine qua non* for providing clients with the services that are the basis of individual political organizations. Consequently, the relative autonomy of the political elite from the broader society has come to mean freedom of action for the Presidency.

The President's autonomy is also enhanced by other factors in Brazilian politics. Most Congressmen reach a position in national politics only after a period of building their political organizations from the local and state levels.[25] Their experience consists of the partial views on national issues available from such vantage points. Furthermore, their role has been defined largely in terms of pressing the limited and specific claims of their clients against policies of the executive and the bureaucracy. Consequently, upon reaching national positions they neither see themselves as the originators of policy initiatives—in contrast to their previous reactive role—nor do they have sufficient perspective on general policy questions and the interlocking of different areas to do so.[26] Hence the Congress has been in no position to challenge the President in policy formulation and has been placed in the weak tactical position of reacting to his initiatives, administrative decrees, and *faits accomplis*.

The power of the Presidency in economic policy issues is all the more noteworthy in light of the President's weakness in some

[25] An exception to what follows here is the case of some intellectuals who are elected to Congress by being given safe districts by some political parties, particularly the PTB, in an effort to raise the party's prestige in elite opinion. The number of such Congressmen has been relatively small, however.

[26] In a similar interpretation of a different situation, Guy Pauker has remarked on the fact that the Indonesian military leaders were trained primarily with the tactical perspective of battalion leaders, without general strategic views, as one of the reasons for their long hesitancy to offer a broad challenge to Sukarno. See his "The Role of the Military in Indonesia," in John J. Johnson (ed.), *The Role of the Military in Underdeveloped Countries* (Princeton, N.J., 1962), pp. 198–199.

of the other arenas of Brazilian politics. During the postwar period Brazilian presidents sometimes lacked legitimacy; and two presidents were in fact excluded from office because of their difficulties in the prestige or in the constitutional arenas. Nevertheless, power in economic policy-making was centralized in the government, where it could be controlled by the President. In reflection of this centralized structure, our discussion—like the accounts of Brazilian political interviewees—has focused so much on "the government." This is, of course, the "State" referred to by the political theorists of other countries in which groups from the broader society also lack substantial influence in the decision-making process.

Effects of Clientelistic Politics

The insulation of the government from political pressures emanating from the broader society, in turn, has had important consequences. Since the government is not oriented or forced into its decisions by outside political pressures, the President's personal preferences count for a great deal in policy formulation. We saw an example of this in the extremely large allocations for the construction of Brasília, a project which owed its existence largely to the strong personal support of the President. Moreover, since the President does not live in personal isolation, the composition of his circle of friends and advisors assumes major political significance.[27] In such a system, clique politics within the Presidential entourage can become very important for policy decisions.

Another important effect of this political system lies in the type of policies formulated. Decisions made in a situation of active group participation in policy-making may be very different from the decisions taken with a degree of insulation from group pressures. Other observers of patronage politics have also noted that such a system can free the government from external political pressures and give it a substantial degree of autonomy.[28]

[27] This is not to say that the cronies of a leader do not have important influence in other political systems. Elsewhere, however, their influence is mitigated by the power of other significant political actors such as legislative committees, interest groups, and political parties.
[28] Meyerson and Banfield, pp. 285–303.

Whether more rational policy emerges than in a decision-making process which is more open to extra-governmental forces depends on the factors which, in practice, do orient the government. We will consider these in the next chapter.

Before proceeding to that discussion, however, we should note how the Brazilian economic policy-making process differs from the pattern that has developed in Mexico. Concluding a study of Mexico addressed to many of the questions that we have considered in Brazil, Raymond Vernon has written:

> The presidents of Mexico have gradually been eased . . . into a political strait jacket. . . . In a real sense, therefore, the strength of the Mexican president is a mirage. True, he need not worry about tripping over a recalcitrant Congress, being blocked by a stubborn minister, or being declared out of bounds by an independent court. But . . . in his concern to extend the reach of the *PRI* the full distance to both the right and the left, he is held to a course of action which is zigzagging and vacillating when it is not blandly neutral.[29]

Paradoxically, the situation of a government without the political autonomy to deal vigorously with economic problems occurs in a country with a strong single-party system, in which the ruling party has a virtual monopoly of political power. During the period we are considering, Brazil offers a twofold contrast with Mexico. Opposition groups had much greater possibilities for attaining power through the electoral process than would be conceivable under PRI dominance in Mexico. At the same time, the Brazilian President, once chosen, has had much greater political autonomy in economic policy than the description just cited indicates for Mexico.

Although Brazilian economic policy-making, with the Executive in a strong central role, may appear fairly similar to authoritarian systems of some other underdeveloped countries, we should note two important differences. During this period, free elections were permitted in which the large middle strata population could express their political preferences; opposition candidates could and did win elections, including the Presidency. Second, the mass media and particularly the newspapers were also free of government control and were able to offer violent criticism of govern-

[29] Raymond Vernon, *The Dilemma of Mexico's Development* (Cambridge, Mass., 1963), pp. 188–189.

ment decisions and indeed of the whole system of clientelist politics. Because of the integrating effects of the prevailing economic
ideology, however, the political elite, the political communications process, and the broader population usually moved together
on economic policy issues.

Brazil's system of clientelistic politics also has some general
implications for the analysis of political development. The failure
of interest groups to play a strong political role is especially noteworthy if we bear in mind that, in contrast with some countries
of Asia or Africa, Brazil is a relatively complex society, with a
high degree of socioeconomic differentiation. During the postwar
period, industry contributed approximately 25 percent of GNP,
and the modern tertiary sector accounted for another 15 percent.
Manufacturing, commercial, and export-agriculture interest
groups with their own power base and political organization had
been operating for at least six decades.

Furthermore, in terms of Brazil's own historical evolution,
sustained industrialization and urbanization have led to a large
increase in the percentage of the population in the middle
stratum. Table 18 presents some rough estimates of changes in

TABLE 18. *Social Class Distribution in Brazil*

Percentage of Population in:	1920	1950	1955
Upper class and upper-middle class	3.5%	5.0%	6.0%
Lower-middle and upper-lower class	26.5	45.0	52.0
Lower-lower class	70.0	50.0	42.0
	100.0	100.0	100.0

Source. These figures are recalculated from data in Robert
Havighurst and J. Roberto Moreira, *Society and Education
in Brazil* (Pittsburgh, Pa., 1965), p. 99. Their material, in turn,
was calculated from the 1920 and 1950 Census of Occupations
and 1955 data from the Social Security Institutes.

Brazilian social class distribution. These figures indicate that the
percentage of the population in the lowest order has declined
sharply, while more than half of the population is in the middle

stratum. Urbanization, literacy and communications—other conditions often associated with the spread of reciprocal power relationships—have also increased markedly.

All this contrasts with the situation in some other less-developed countries, with a smaller middle group and with less socioeconomic differentiation. This is perhaps the most noteworthy feature of the Brazilian situation. The scene seems to have been set for a system in which groups from the broader society take a major political role, influencing and constraining government action. Instead, the politicians have attained considerable autonomy and, except for the case of the military, have greatly reduced the bargaining power of other socioeconomic groups.

The Brazilian experience is also worth noting as a possible mode of long-term political development. Brazil's success in centralizing power for effective economic policy-making appears all the more interesting since it was achieved without the extensive bloodshed that occurred, for example, in Mexico's political modernization. From accounts of Brazilian politics in the period 1890–1929, although the professional politicians had a considerable role even then, the country seems to have been fairly close to a system of interest-group politics. This was a special kind of group politics, for all participants had to be of upper status. Within this framework, however, private groups such as the coffee planters and the industrialists seem to have exerted much more influence than they have in more recent years.[30] Indeed, from the way the political activities of one important group, the cotton textile manufacturers, have been described, they reached the peak of their power in the late 1920's.[31] As this indicates, the

[30] One noteworthy episode occurred in 1905. The likely government nominee for the Presidency, Bernardino de Campos, was forced to retire his candidacy after a newspaper interview in which he opposed undervaluation of the exchange rate, a measure supported by the industrialists and the coffee planters. See Nícia Vilela Luz, *A Luta pela Industrialização do Brasil* (São Paulo, 1961), pp. 181–183. Contrary to what has sometimes been maintained, there had been substantial industrial development in Brazil, and not only in textiles, by the first decade of this century. Both points are documented in my "Note on Brazilian Economic Development before 1939" (mimeo, 1967).
[31] Stanley J. Stein, *The Brazilian Cotton Textile Manufacture* (Cambridge, Mass., 1957), pp. 123–128, 247.

Brazilian case does not conform to models which see the political
change accompanying industrialization as a secular trend of expanding participation by organized interest groups in the policy-
making process.

Economic development introduced a new complexity to Brazilian society, and increased the number of significant potential
participants. Economic and social change also weakened the
power of once-dominant elites. In this process, the new middle
strata have gained a greater political voice, principally through
the public opinion we will discuss in the next chapter. The operation of clientelistic politics, however, enabled the politicians to
limit the impact of new groups' entry and participation in politics. This experience underscores the obvious point that even
under nontotalitarian conditions, industrial expansion and a sharp
rise in many of the indices of political mobilization may not lead
to an increase in reciprocal power relations.

Our discussion also has some methodological implications.
The citation from V. O. Key is a useful reminder that clientelistic and personalistic politics may be two sides of the same
coin.[32] The personalist aspects of Brazilian politics have long
been stressed; but emphasis on cultural and psychological conditions should not divert attention from the structural features
which give scope to their operation.

The suggestion that a model of patronage politics may be
most useful for the study of national economic policy-making in
Brazil also has analytical implications; for it contrasts with the
conceptual frameworks more commonly employed. Social scientists from the advanced countries, when discussing Brazilian politics, have often worked within an interest-group framework,
whereas Latin American analysts generally employ a neo-Marxist,
class-struggle model.[33] Such approaches entail the assumption
that these groups actually have significant political power,
and that political relations are conditioned by this structure.
If, as I have suggested, these groups are too weakened by
the system of clientelistic politics to play a strong role, and their

[32] See n. 19 above.
[33] The phenomenon of *clientelismo* has been widely noted, but not its implications for permitting a greater measure of autonomy and, perhaps,
rationality.

power in the policy-making process may be largely a myth, a class or interest-group conceptual framework is much less relevant than in other countries.[34] By the same token, the political elite and its internal interaction deserve much more attention than in systems where they can be considered a mere reflection of more basic socioeconomic forces. This methodological implication of the Brazilian cause may also be relevant for the study of politics in other transitional societies.[35] Finally, if group pressures do not have such influence, we must identify and study the factors that *do* determine government decision-making in such a system. We turn to these in the next chapter.

[34] Such myths derived from ideological perspective may themselves have important political effects. One example occurred in Brazil in late 1963 and early 1964. Many political participants believed that the trade unions and the "working class" had the resources to make a real bid for power. This generalized belief had important political consequences, both in encouraging President Goulart toward less centrist solutions and in prompting the military toward a political takeover. In April 1964, however, any such "working-class" movement came to nothing.

[35] Although there are some significant differences (most notably the integrating structure of the Congress Party), we should note some important parallels between the conclusions reached above and those of Myron Weiner's study of organized business in India, in *The Politics of Scarcity* (Chicago, Ill., 1963). He too concludes that although intellectuals often claim that "the class that rules India today, the paramount power, is the Indian bourgeoisie" (p. 101, n. 3), in fact "the influence [of organized business] on central government policy is negligible" (p. 129). Power in reality rests in the hands of the professional politicians (p. 102). Furthermore, "Indian business operates in the framework of the government's ideology" (p. 128); its position has been greatly weakened by suspicion of its "selfish" motives (pp. 123-128); and it acts largely in an effort to modify specifics of policies decided by government (p. 119). For this purpose, the most effective technique has been technical research for influencing the government within its own framework (pp. 122-123).

CHAPTER 8

Elite Opinion, Ideology, and the *Técnicos*

As might be expected in a system where decisions are not determined by political pressures from the broader society, the bureaucracy and elite opinion, following both ideology and less formalized attitudes, are very important in the policy-making process.[1]

Elite Opinion

One force whose influence we often noted in our case studies is elite opinion. Our references, however, are no more frequent than those made by Brazilian politicians, government officials, and interest-group representatives in discussing how and why economic policy decisions were made in Brazil. When discussing policy formation, *a opinião pública* is usually cited as a determining factor. We also noted the prominence of press campaigns as a technique used by interest groups to influence government action. The power of the communications process was demonstrated perhaps most dramatically in the newspaper campaign that isolated President Getúlio Vargas from the political elite and drove him to end his career in suicide.

A detailed study of the Brazilian political communications process is not now available, and such a project is beyond the scope of this book. Having singled out its crucial importance,

[1] It should be stressed again that we are dealing here only with *economic* policy-making. Brazilian politics in other areas may well be different. For example, much more intra-elite conflict appears to take place in the arena where prestige and position are disputed among the politicians. The main differences seem to lie in the integrating effects of the economic ideology discussed below and in the unitary form in which economic policy issues have been formulated politically.

however, let us advance some tentative generalizations on how elite opinion operates, why it is so powerful, and what are some of its political consequences.

From the narratives of Brazilian political interviewees, it appears that the "public opinion" referred to so often has two components. The first, which we have called "elite opinion," consists of the ideas circulating among the higher echelons of the bureaucracy, the politicians, military officers, and the journalists directing the leading mass media, particularly the newspapers of Rio de Janeiro. Leaders of the principal interest groups and prominent industrialists also participate, though apparently much less than the political and communications elites themselves. Other channels, such as the professional clubs of the military officers, industrialists, and engineers, are also connected to the principal network, though they seem to receive more messages than they transmit. Direct interpersonal contacts, which may be organized through cliques, clubs, or around particular occupations and institutions, appear to be at the heart of the communications process. The mass media, and particularly the newspapers, however, play a key role by providing a general framework for discussion. They are also in the strategic position of being the only channel that encompasses all of the face-to-face networks.[2]

Second, there is what may be called "middle strata opinion"—the attitudes of the urban middle and (literate) lower classes and their media. Together, elite and middle strata opinion form the broad communications network of public opinion. Though the links are hard to pinpoint, elite opinion and middle strata opinion are connected.[3] As a result, middle strata opinion does have some influence on elite opinion. This feature is also important both for providing important boundaries on the entire system of public opinion and for limiting the rate at which it can move in changing its ideas.

By all accounts, the President and the great newspapers of Rio

---

[2] Description and analysis of the system's communications flows are difficult and subject to a bias because only the newspapers leave a written and public record. I have tried to guard against this bias in the subsequent discussion, but it may be worthwhile to stress again that face-to-face communication seems to be at the heart of the system.

[3] It should be borne in mind that this connection is often exaggerated, and what is termed public opinion is often really elite opinion.

de Janeiro take the dominant role in leading elite opinion.[4] The President has this position because of his other sources of power, which make his orientations particularly important. The "prestige papers" of Rio also have a key role both in originating and in transmitting many of the messages entering elite opinion.[5] Although these newspapers are by no means politically neutral, they are not permanently linked with particular parties, factions, or interest groups, but rather maintain a position of independent critique. This tradition of autonomy greatly enhances their prestige and influence, for they appear as one of the few political actors confronting the nation's problems without partisan motives, which, as noted earlier, Brazilian political culture considers corrupt.[6]

Within the newspapers themselves, the professional journalists seem to have the dominant position. Although the intelligentsia as a group has a part in originating the ideas that feed into the communications system, its impact is indirect and diffuse rather than direct. University professors do not appear to have a key role as opinion leaders. This function is assumed by prominent intellectuals working as journalists, administrators, or politicians and by leading members of the political elite, particularly the President and his entourage.

Finally the Brazilian communications process is apparently not very compartmentalized or segmented along lines of different socioeconomic groups. Apart from the broad demarcation between elite and middle strata opinion, the only exception is the military, who have maintained their own opinion-leading institu-

[4] The principal newspapers which take the lead in this process are the Rio de Janeiro *Correio da Manha* and *O Jornal do Brasil*. To a much lesser extent in *national* politics, and in a very different vein, *O Estado de São Paulo* plays a similar role in São Paulo.

[5] The term is from the study by Ithiel de Sola Pool et al., *The "Prestige Papers"* (Stanford, Cal., 1952). As the authors of that work put it (p. 83): "The prestige paper . . . assures widespread dissemination to the elite of policy-relevant information and attitudes." In Brazil, these newspapers have a more independent and influential role. This contrast with the developed political systems studied by Pool probably stems from the greater importance of parties and interest groups in the developed countries.

[6] My comments on the political autonomy of the newspapers applies only to the specific periodicals cited. Other Brazilian newspapers may be more open to economic and political pressures. This difference introduces the possibility for divergence between elite and middle strata opinion, with important political consequences.

tion and their own internal lines of communication. Within the rest of the elite, however, ideas flow relatively easily within one unified network.

Reasons for the Influence of Elite Opinion

Elite opinion has such compelling influence largely because of the system of clientelist politics. First, the influence derives from the absence of determining *political* pressures from the broader society. To illustrate: if the power of the Congress, the interest groups, and the states in American politics were to be drastically curtailed through a strong central authority, the influence of the Washington climate of opinion would greatly increase.

Moreover, as noted earlier, the most important actors in Brazilian politics are professional politicians. These men spend the greater part of their time away from their region of origin, in the political capitals of Rio de Janeiro and Brasília. As clientelistic politicians, they are under no necessity to receive communications of outlook and expertise from outside socioeconomic groups. Consequently, the only messages necessarily reaching the politicians are those originating within their own occupational milieu and the Rio newspapers. In more formal terms, when vertical channels of communication connecting the political elite and the rest of the society are relatively few and weak, the influence of lateral, intra-elite channels becomes much more compelling.

The newspapers are also accorded special respect because of their tradition of political independence and broad perspective on national issues. Indeed, in a system without strong political parties that aggregate interests and provide a degree of coherence among individual issues, the newspapers are one of the few political actors whose perspective encompasses the problems of the country as a whole.[7] The newspapers also have a special advan-

---

[7] Cf. similar comments by Banfield and Wilson, *City Politics* (Cambridge, Mass., 1965), p. 313, in their discussion of the power of the press in a similar political structure: "The . . . newspaper is one of the very few major actors on the civic scene (the mayor or city manager [in our context, the President] is usually the only other) in a position both to take a comprehensive view of the public interest and to exercise a powerful influence. It is therefore a political institution of great importance."

tage for influence because they are in the unique situation of having direct access to the entire political elite.

Furthermore, because of the inadequacies of other political organizations, Brazil's large middle strata groups lack sustained representation in the political process. Nevertheless, they *are* there, both at elections and in between—if only as potential participants in the country's political life. Because of the weakness of other mediating institutions, public opinion may be their most authentic political expression.[8] Since elite opinion is believed to be connected with and to speak, at least in part, for the broader society, it has special influence among the politicians, who are concerned not to lose contact with the electorate. Even though the connection between elite and middle strata opinion may be exaggerated and, on some issues, spurious, such a procedure for gauging the distribution of political support is by no means irrational.[9] Because of the power of the press in molding voter attitudes, an ex post congruence between the views of the newspapers and of the broader public may well emerge even though it did not exist originally.

POLITICAL CONSEQUENCES OF THE INFLUENCE OF ELITE OPINION

The special influence of the political communications process has had important consequences for Brazilian policy-making. First, at any point in time elite opinion constitutes a field of forces conditioning and constraining decision-making. As we saw in our case studies, this factor is by no means completely determining, but leaves room for maneuver, not least in leading elite opinion itself. Possibilities for freedom of action exist, however, only *within the framework* of elite views. These allow for ma-

[8] Because of the importance of public opinion as a major channel for political representation, issues to which public opinion has rallied vigorously constitute the most important political achievement of the middle strata. An example is the government petroleum company, Petrobrás. In this perspective, expanded public-sector economic activity rather than, for example, more vigorous parliamentary institutions is one of the principal political consequences of the middle strata's growth in Brazil.
[9] For a similar phenomenon in the United States, see Richard R. Fagen, *Politics and Communication* (Boston, Mass., 1966), p. 51. The possible distortions introduced by reliance on this "public opinion" are much greater in Brazil, however, because fewer alternative channels of vertical communication are available than in the United States.

neuver, but they cannot be disregarded. For example, in a somewhat similar system, Peron's Argentina, even the dictator found that he could not move too abruptly to grant the international oil companies a place in the Argentine economy. Peron's moves in this direction were too radical for an insufficiently prepared elite opinion, and played an important part in his downfall.

Furthermore, the communications system is not neutral in the problems it chooses to perceive and in the way it structures them for decision-making. We saw an example of its crucial mediating effects in the selection of direct foreign investment as one of the country's highest-priority problems in the early 1960's, as well as in the special way in which the issue was approached. As this episode indicates, the political communications system creates a world unto itself for the policy-making process. This may or may not approximate objective reality.

Moreover, even less than in many other systems, ideas are not considered on their intrinsic merits, but rather on the degree to which they accord with the political elite's a priori conceptions and emotional predispositions. The contrast here is with countries in which the political elite is not so well insulated from political pressures emanating from the broader society, and is not so free to consider issues within its own special perspective. We noted such a case in the policy-makers' perception that the country's balance-of-payments problem could be dealt with only by import substitution and the persistent neglect of the possibilities offered by export expansion.

Finally, the importance of the communications process makes of the press an important political actor to be reckoned with in its own right. Brazilian Presidents have recognized this explicitly, as noted in Chapter 3, by allocating the newspapers preferential exchange-rate treatment for newsprint imports. This policy is in marked contrast with the relatively *poor* import treatment usually accorded newspapers in less-developed countries.[10] Moreover, the key role of the journalists in the communications process gives a special political importance to these intellectuals who create and transmit the ideas entering into elite opinion.

[10] See Ithiel de Sola Pool, "The Mass Media in the Modernization Process," in Lucian W. Pye (ed.), *Communications and Political Development* (Princeton, N.J., 1963), p. 235.

Since most Brazilian intellectuals are "nationalists," the views and symbols of this particular ideology are given preferential political access, with important effects on the tone and outlook of Brazilian politics.

The importance of elite opinion makes it a prime target for private interests attempting to influence the government, and reintroduces the possibility of a strong political position for business groups. The independence of the prestige papers from financial pressures, and the political elite's resistance to the cruder forms of communications manipulation, however, do not permit the industrialists an easy opportunity for influence. Their difficulties have been increased because the ideology which dominates the communications media often conflicts with proposals advanced by the industrialists, while, for reasons discussed earlier, there is no predisposition to defer to the views of private groups.

Finally, the importance of elite opinion makes it a key point for leverage and change in Brazilian policy-making. Precisely because this decision-making process is not so closely constrained by political structure, shifts within elite opinion can have disproportionate political effects.

Some other consequences have followed from the fact that from the early postwar years to the period 1962–1963 a single network dominated the Brazilian political communications process. This led to a homogenization of viewpoints within the political elite greater than within Brazilian society as a whole. The attitudes which the politicians shared probably mediated and reduced conflict. The dominance of the single communications network was also important in socializing the leaders of the new political groups into the views held by participants already established within the system. For example, leaders of the trade unions— when they are not themselves politicians delegated by the President—were brought into Brazilian politics with views on economic policy not very different from those of the industrialists and the professional politicians. Such a development contrasts with a situation like that in France under the Third Republic, where because of different structural conditions, the industrial workers and their leaders remained outside of the central communications network. As a result, they approached policy questions with views so different from those of other participants that they posed a serious threat to the stability and working efficiency of the ongoing system.

Elite opinion, in turn, has viewed economic issues through the special prism of an economic ideology, to which we now turn.

The Ideology

Any outside observer of postwar Brazilian economic policy-making cannot fail to be struck by the special way in which many issues were approached. Important assumptions, attitudes, and even "data" were taken so much for granted that there was little discussion of such "self-evident" truths. This is perhaps the best indication for the prevalence of a widely held ideology.

This ideology, similar to economic views common in many other less-developed countries during the 1940's and 1950's, has several basic themes.[11] First, it has stressed the importance of re-structuring Brazil's traditionally agricultural economy and reducing the country's dependence on the world economy for supply of most manufactured products. Pointing to the sharp decline in national income which Brazil suffered after the 1929 collapse of world coffee prices, the ideology has emphasized the dangers of Brazil's remaining mainly an exporter of primary products. The experience in World War II, when shipping difficulties prevented Brazil from attaining desired levels of imports, further underlined the possible dangers of dependence on the world economy.

Industrialization has been seen as the way out of this situation, both to reduce the country's dependence on foreign trade conditions and to create a modern economy. Aside from the desire to emulate the advanced countries, pressures to demonstrate competence in modern technology have been also a central motif. In these respects, the ideology has often focused more on national achievement and economic modernization than on raising per capita income.[12]

---

[11] This resemblance, notably to the views elaborated by Raúl Prebisch and the United Nations Economic Commission for Latin America, seems to have been the result of parallel development because of similar experience, rather than direct influence or borrowing.

[12] This was brought out graphically in an interview with a prominent Brazilian economic administrator. When asked whether he would prefer a situation in which the economy grew at a 7 percent annual rate based on

As we saw earlier, the ideology has attributed crucial importance to development of "basic industries" to provide domestic supply of steel, petroleum, and chemicals. These industries possess the multiple virtues of promoting the development of the entire economy—and preventing growth from being retarded by adverse import conditions—and of being industries of "complex technology" where Brazilians could demonstrate modern skills. Because development of these industries might be beyond the capabilities of private entrepreneurs, and to facilitate expulsion of foreign capital from such strategic industries, the ideology has accorded an ample role to the public sector in the promotion of Brazilian development.

As suggested earlier, this ideology appears to be based on two components. First, it contains elements of an implicit model of economic development. The emphasis on immediate and anticipatory import substitution, for example, reflects the intuitive conception of an economy whose growth encounters a rising real cost of marginal imports as a result of export conditions assumed to be stagnant. The emphasis on economic infrastructure and the "basic industries" stems from a perception of the importance of potential external economies and diseconomies for growth. Similarly, many of the long-term investments to which the ideology led reflected an effort to overcome various capital-market imperfections which were felt to be distorting resource allocation.[13]

These conceptions were generally supported by the nationalistic emotional considerations that were also very much present. These are apparent in the drive to overcome difficulties imposed

expansion of the textile industry, or a 3 percent rate based on expansion of the steel industry, he unhesitatingly chose 3 percent. The 7 percent case, he explained, would not be "real" development.

[13] This is seen most clearly in the creation of the National Development Bank to provide long-term investment funds whose prior unavilability, because of the underdeveloped condition of the domestic capital market, it was felt, had deterred Brazilians from investing in long-range activities. Public-sector investment in steel and other capital-intensive products reflected a similar effort, in this case by direct appropriation of investment resources, to overcome divergences between social and private returns and investment horizons. The establishment of government credit institutions to provide loans for various agricultural products and the creation of various regional development funds were other attempts to offset institutional barriers leading to an imperfect allocation of credit by commodity or by region.

by the balance-of-payments (sometimes referred to as "the external strangle-hold"); the effort to assert Brazilian capabilities in modern activities; the fear of foreign dominance of the domestic economy; and dependence on foreign sources of supply. As the frequent references to the danger of "dependence" suggest, political and psychological factors are central to the ideology—the desire to avoid inferiority and colonial status.[14]

The ideology's economic views have been virtually uncontested in Brazil since at least the early 1950's. The ideology has been so pervasive partly because it has had almost no competition as an interpretation of Brazilian reality and the possibilities for action. First, the debacle of the 1930's demonstrated the dangers of excessive reliance on export agriculture, and conclusively discredited the export interests and their rejection of industrialization as an approach to the country's economic problems. Their views had previously been questioned by the modernizing intelligentsia; now they lost their prestige in wider circles and were simultaneously deprived of their political support. Decline of the traditional export-producers in national politics was one condition for the new consensus; failure of the industrialist group to develop an independent ideology was another.[15] As mentioned earlier, in contrast with, say, the United States, Brazilian indus-

[14] To my knowledge, no psychoanalytic interpretation of Brazilian nationalist ideology has been done. Considering the frequent emphasis on dependence, on things "basic," and the fear of foreign penetration, such a study may well be worthwhile. Concerning the significance here attributed to political factors in this economic ideology, cf. David Landes, "Japan and Europe: Contrasts in Industrialization," in William P. Lockwood (ed.), *The State and Economic Enterprise in Japan* (Princeton, N.J., 1965), esp. pp. 137–150 for a similar emphasis on what he calls "the primacy of the political" as the motive force for modernization in Japan and Germany.

[15] In the 1930's and 1940's, Roberto Simonsen did attempt, almost single-handedly, to formulate a private-sector industrialist ideology of Brazilian economic development. His views coincided in great measure with those of the modernizing intelligentsia, however, and he also went along on key points of possible divergence, for example, on the need for extensive government intervention in the economy and "planning." In instances where his views did conflict with the more pervasive ideology, such as in his call for giving existing industries priority in investment allocations, his views were simply ignored, and the private-sector ideology of development disappeared in the mainstream of the intelligentsia's views. On these points, see Warren Dean, pp. 135–140, *São Paulo's Industrial Elite, 1890–1960* (Ph.D. dissertation, University of Florida, 1964).

trialists have not had their own special interpretation of the country's economic problems and how to deal with them. As a result, they have not offered a doctrinal or programmatic alternative but have been incorporated without a challenge into the prevailing views.

Finally, Brazil's economic intelligentsia also presented no critique or alternative to the ideology. To be sure, there were controversies among Brazilian economists concerning some issues. To an outside observer, however, what is most striking is the agreement on the general approach;[16] and the points that were accepted without question by all participants were much more important than those under debate.[17] For example, the possibility of giving greater importance to exportation was never given more than lip-service, and the strategy of development based upon industrialization was never questioned.[18] True critics, who took issue with some of the ideology's fundamental assumptions, were isolated, and labeled as subversive and probably corrupted by foreign interests. To speak of expanded exports was not only unfashionable but unpatriotic. As a result of the widespread acceptance of the ideology, Brazilian development policy was made in a framework of consensus on major issues.

This ideological consensus served to orient Brazilian policymakers in identifying economic problems and structuring possible solutions. Consequently, unlike some less-developed countries, the absence of determining political pressures did not lead Brazil to a situation of anomie and inaction in policy formulation. Because of the ideology, there were no debates in Brazil on such issues as industrial versus agricultural development; heavy versus

---

[16] Frank Bonilla makes a similar point: "Thus in examining the substantial output of Brazilian nationalist writing, the reader can miss the underlying unity of ideas by focusing on the surface fragmentation. . . . There is a fair degree of consensus about what is desired for the nation." "A National Ideology for Development: Brazil," in Kalman Silvert (ed.), *Expectant Peoples* (New York, 1963), p. 235.

[17] Although some of the disagreements were violent, the metaphor of a tempest in a teacup suggests itself—great agitation within narrowly circumscribed boundaries.

[18] See pp. 173–178 for a discussion of some of the reasons for the lack of criticism of the views underlying Brazilian economic policy-making.

light industry; or import substitution versus export promotion. Indeed, consensus on economic policy was so great as to stifle what might often have been fruitful debate and choice among alternatives. However, it did have the positive function of getting decision-making rapidly off-center on fundamental issues, and giving a stable orientation to economic policy.

The widespread acceptance of the ideology also facilitated effective decision-making within its framework. Brazilian politics have often been cited for its problem-solving style, in contrast with more ideologically oriented political cultures.[19] This pragmatic approach, however, operated only *within* the framework of the ideology. There it was possible only because of the consensus and the consequent delimitation of issues and solutions. Finally, ideological consensus greatly reduced the political conflict surrounding the resolution of economic policy issues—both within the government and as between the government and private groups. Because of the ideology's integrating effects, even functional and regional groups which were not benefiting directly from allocation policies, and which may have had conflicting interests accepted the legitimacy of government decisions.

The ideology could take programmatic form and effective relevance for policy-making, however, only because there were administrators who could make it operational for implementation. This depended on changes in the pattern of recruitment and training for the administrative elite.

The Técnicos

Determining a locus of significant political power is a difficult task, but in the course of interviews it became clear that the professional administrators in the government economic agencies played a key role in Brazilian economic policy.

Interviews showed that the administrators had considerable

[19] See Frank Bonilla's observation: "Brazil is a nation of pragmatists. Unembarrassed by rigid commitment to ideas or principles . . ." in Silvert, p. 232. As in the United States, an ideology which was so pervasive as to permit consensus on issues of principle facilitated programmatic action and a pragmatic style.

autonomy in dealing with the policy issues arising in their agencies. Often they made important decisions without consulting congressmen or interest-group representatives. They also took considerable initiative in structuring the issues for policy action, by technical studies delineating problem areas and frameworks for their solution.

Another noteworthy feature is the extent to which professional administrators have been appointed to the command posts in the key economic agencies and occasionally even to the post of Finance Minister. This is quite different from a pattern such as that of the United States. There, these positions are usually filled by "political" nominees designated by the interest groups or political parties, while the professional administrator has at most advisor status, to be heeded or not at the discretion of the appointee brought in from outside the bureaucracy. In our case studies we also saw evidence of the administrators' power in the fact that interest groups attempting to influence government policy consider them a prime target for petition. The power of the *técnicos*, particularly the economists, is reflected in the joke cited by insiders to Brazilian economic policy-making: that all Brazilian economists have a "Keynes complex": born commoners, they want to die lords.

These indications of the administrators' power in economic policy formulation suggest that they have developed as a significant elite in this area of Brazilian politics. Before we go on to discuss the reasons for and the effects of their power, let us consider who are these *técnicos*—"experts"—as they are called in Brazil.[20]

THE EMERGENCE OF THE *Técnicos*

The *técnicos* are a group of economist and engineer administrators holding high positions in the Monetary Authority, the Development Bank, the Foreign Exchange, Credit, and Rediscount Departments of the *Banco do Brasil,* and the various government agencies and public corporations dealing with such in-

---

[20] The appellation has the connotation of apolitical technical specialist, *not* of "technocrat."

dustries as steel, automobiles, and petroleum.[21] In the early 1960's the group numbered perhaps 40 officials. Economists have tended to predominate in the agencies dealing with monetary and foreign-exchange policy; engineers have been prominent in investment policy and production activities.

Most of the *técnicos* are relatively young men, born in the years 1920–1925, although there was an earlier, much smaller group born in the first decade of the century and reaching important positions by the late 1930's. In terms of their geographical origins, they come from all over Brazil, though São Paulo State is heavily underrepresented.[22] Some are descendants of immigrants, but Brazilians coming from families of longer residence in the country predominate. In terms of their socioeconomic origins, most of these men are sons of the urban "middle sectors": the civil service, the military, the liberal professions—particularly medicine and engineering—and some commercial activities. When these people do come from rural areas, their families were usually engaged in marketing rather than in agricultural production. One surprising aspect of the group's socioeconomic origins is the number who have come from fairly low status.

The process by which the new elite has emerged is also interesting. With the 1929 coffee collapse, continuing rapid industrialization, and an expanded public-sector role in the economy, the Brazilian government was confronted with many new and complex tasks which required specialized technical knowledge. These

[21] Paragraphs that follow are based on interviews with government economic administrators. In order to avoid a formal prying into antecedents, a written questionnaire was not used.

[22] The reason usually given for this is that São Paulo personnel have been attracted to careers in the private sector because of the rapid economic growth of São Paulo. This pattern fits in with a study of Spain by Juan Linz and Armando de Miguel, "Within-Nation Differences and Comparisons: The Eight Spains," in Richard L. Merritt and Stein Rokkan (eds.), *Comparing Nations: The Use of Quantitative Data in Cross-National Research* (New Haven, 1966). They report that the regions in Spain which have not industrialized rapidly have had differentially higher rates of recruitment to the upper administrative elite. As suggested earlier, the potential conflict built into a situation where one region develops economically and the others supply most of the personnel influencing government policy has been mitigated in Brazil by the integrating effects of the economic ideology.

involved both immediate policy problems and questions of broader economic perspective.[23] Since very little formal economics was taught in Brazil until the late 1940's, a premium was placed upon individuals able to perform the necessary tasks. Engineers could undertake some of these functions since they could deal with the technical and sometimes quantitative aspects of analysis.[24] Some administrators also mastered the necessary material on their own, sometimes with subsequent study abroad through international training programs. In both cases, under the new demands individuals of diverse socioeconomic background could rise high in the civil service on the basis of their capabilities in the new technical skills.

The rise of the *técnicos* also owes much to the spread of universalistic criteria for advancement. Under the pressure for better quality performance and the example of administrative practice in the advanced countries, in the late 1930's first the *Banco do Brasil* and then the federal civil service (with the formation of a Civil Service Commission, the DASP) introduced systems of promotion by merit and examination. (At the same time, the opportunities for patronage appointments *also* increased with the rapid expansion of the public sector, particularly the social security *Institutos*.) As a result, individuals with ability were able to reach positions of high status and responsibility which would have been unthinkable for persons of their social origins under the previous regime.

The emergence of this new elite was further facilitated by the institution-building that has accompanied Brazilian development. In the early 1940's a few nationalist economist-intellectuals con-

[23] The need for broader economic perspective placed a few *técnicos* in the role of policy-making advisers to the President. An early example was the relation of Rómulo de Almeida to Getúlio. What I have in mind through most of the subsequent discussion, however, is the *técnicos* in the role of policy-making *administrators*, in which their influence, albeit more subtle, was much more pervasive.

[24] Concerning the prominent role of engineers in economic policy formation, we should add that the Brazilian engineering schools always taught some economics. The professional self-definition of Brazilian engineers also tends to be much broader than, for example, is the case with engineers in the United States. In the discussion forums of their professional clubs and in their journals, general issues of national economic policy are often raised.

cerned with improving the quality of economic policy formulation and administration prevailed on the President to found the Getúlio Vargas Foundation, as an institute for personnel training, data collection, and economic analysis. As its name and antecedents indicate, the Foundation was at that time part of the general thrust for national modernization promoted under Getúlio Vargas, and it was to serve as an institutional base in the careers of many of the *técnicos*. Subsequently, the newly founded Monetary Authority (SUMOC) and National Development Bank also provided strategic places within the government where these individuals could develop their careers and their influence on policy. Creation of these new institutions dealing with policy of the highest priority saved the *técnicos* the years of struggle that would have been necessary to take over the older agencies and oust their personnel from key positions in the decision-making process.

The *técnicos* show considerable self-awareness of themselves as a political elite and a group with similar orientations. To be sure, they have sometimes been more concerned with factional conflicts than with their general homogeneity. In the early 1960's, the group was split into two factions, one "structuralist" (under the intellectual leadership of Celso Furtado) and another "monetarist" (of which Roberto Campos was the principal spokesman).[25] As these appellations indicate, an important divergence existed between the two groups in their interpretation of the Brazilian inflation. They also differed in their attitude toward direct foreign investment and, perhaps, on the scope for fruitful government intervention in the economy. These differences partly reflect the usual conflict between administrators with the clashing role requirements of the Monetary Authority and the Development Bank, though personal political orientation and temperament also played an important part.[26] More important than these

[25] Perhaps another group of "true nationalists" taking more extreme positions in their opposition to foreign capital should also be included. A rough approximation of the distribution of the *técnicos* in March 1964 as between the three groups might be: 70 percent in the Celso Furtado group; 15 percent in the Roberto Campos group; and 15 percent in the "true nationalists."

[26] These differences do not appear to be systematically related to such factors as differential exposure to foreign study or travel—that is, cosmopolitanism versus nativism—or to different socioeconomic origins.

conflicts, however, was the consensus which transcended the two factions—the commitment to rapid economic development through import-substituting industrialization and the emphasis on the "basic industries"—which gave the group a basic homogeneity.[27] Equally important, the two groups were also able to work together constructively.[28]

SOURCES OF THEIR POWER

As noted in the previous chapter, political power in Brazil has passed into the hands of the professional politicians and particularly to the President. In matters of economic policy, this power has largely been delegated to the *técnicos*.

One important reason for this lies in what we might call the myth of the "technical solution" in Brazilian politics. As mentioned earlier, Brazilian political culture takes an organic view of society and believes that policy-making should be directed to-

[27] These similarities may be seen in a comparison of the two economic plans for which the groups have been responsible: the 1962 Furtado *Plano Trienal* and the 1964 *Programa de Ação Econômica* prepared by Roberto Campos. Although these two plans were prepared under very different governments—in 1964 under a military regime which had deposed the previous President—they do not show great differences on the means and ends of Brazilian economic development or any disposition of one group to reverse priorities and programs of the other. Perhaps the only exception is that the Campos plan looked favorably on entry of direct foreign private investment. This was regarded with considerable reserve by the Furtado group, although they too would have permitted such investment, properly regulated, in some industries. As noted earlier, whatever its emotional impact, the issue is in any case not very important, one way or the other, for Brazilian economic development. The Campos plan also placed more emphasis on price stabilization; but this was largely because the inflation had accelerated rapidly in the interval since 1962, and no one, including Furtado, now claimed that inflation was promoting growth.

[28] For example, it was Roberto Campos who as Director of the National Development Bank invited Celso Furtado to return from ECLA to a post in the Bank, where Furtado prepared his report on the Northeast. This was to serve as the basis for the SUDENE. Similarly, Campos and Furtado both worked together under the Goulart regime (Campos as Ambassador in Washington, Furtado as Planning Minister); and ultimately neither was able to continue under the regime, for Campos resigned, and Furtado retired from national economic policy-making to the SUDENE. The ability of the different wings of *técnicos* to work together and avoid dissipation of their abilities was facilitated by the fact that there were many different government tasks, for which different talents and orientations could be used within the same general framework.

ward finding policies that are best for the community as a whole. Further, it is believed that such solutions can indeed be found if issues are approached in a nonpartisan manner. This attitude is essentially antipolitical. Within this framework, policy formulation by technical experts does not have the antidemocratic implication it may have in other cultures; rather, it appears as the *truly* democratic approach. Such a set of beliefs lends strong support for those purporting to apply an "objective" approach to "the country's" policy problems. Again, an analogy is suggested with the politics of defense policy in the United States. With the conception of a unitary "national interest" and with broad consensus on the ends and means of policy in this area, many important decisions are depoliticized and delegated to the "experts."

Furthermore, because of other conditions in Brazilian politics, there is something of a vacuum in the formulation of general policy. The politicians are engaged primarily in pressing specific claims of their particular clients. Interest groups are discredited and weakened. In part because of clientelist politics, there are no strong political parties to aggregate interests and formulate general programs. Moreover, in Brazilian political culture, the role of considering the economic situation of the country as a whole is allocated to "the government," for interest groups have in practice accepted the role of pleaders for their own limited interests. Hence the Executive has almost no challenge as guardian of the needs of the entire country.

Within the government, the *técnicos* possess a virtual monopoly on the technical knowledge necessary for economic policy formulation. Particularly since World War II, the problems of economic policy in Brazil have become increasingly difficult and complex. The persistent balance-of-payments problem, the inflation, and the commitment to an active investment and production role for the public sector have ended the previous era when common sense and commercial experience were sufficient to manage the country's economic affairs. By professional training, however, the politicians lack the technical knowledge in economics and engineering that would enable them to speak with authority in these policy areas. They have also been unwilling to make the adjustments that would give them technical expertise—for example, by working with professional staff of their own. This seems to stem from their conception of the legislative role, which is a combination of pressing for specific favors and applying general wisdom to the country's "basic" needs rather than doing the job of narrow technicians.[29] Finally, as noted previously, since most congressmen are machine politicians, they lack expertise either from their own experience or from interest-group patrons to orient them in these issues. Consequently, most politicians lack the competence or the self-assurance to deal with economic matters, which remain a mystery to them and in which they delegate responsibility to those with technical training.

The *técnicos* also derive considerable authority from their education because of the high status accorded to intellectual attainments in Brazil. This is a political culture where the first thing said to discredit an opponent is, "He has no education." The educated administrators gain accordingly. Paradoxically, their prestige is increased by a contrasting theme of anti-intellectualism. One aspect of the crisis of the 1930's was a radical rethinking of the country's intellectual tradition. The previous emphasis on "humanistic" and "literary" traditions was questioned, and a conscious shift was undertaken from the "French" intellectual tradition to a more technical "American" approach. This went together with a movement against previous efforts at a merely "political" solution to the country's problems whose proponents, it was alleged, were often salon academics—"divorced from the country's real conditions and needs"—to an attack on the country's "basic" social and economic problems. The engineers and economists rose in status as masters of the technical knowledge necessary for the new political style. Thus they have gained from both the intellectual and the anti-intellectual motifs within Brazilian society.

The *técnicos* have derived additional prestige from the fact that most of them are professional, career administrators with a

---

[29] This is borne out in a personal communication dated October 17, 1966 from Robert Packenham, who has conducted extensive field research among Brazilian congressmen. As he put it: "There is a predisposition among many, if not most Brazilian legislators to shy away from the use of expertise, staff, *técnicos*. There are doubtless many reasons for this, but one of the most striking appears to be imbedded in their notion of a legislator's appropriate role. This is the view that staff expertise might compromise their competence and integrity as wise generalists. . . ."

general reputation for honesty in office. This enables them to speak with heightened moral authority in a political culture which believes strongly that public affairs should be managed with probity but that the politicians and interest groups are tainted with corruption. These considerations making for prestige and moral stature are especially important for power in a system, such as the Brazilian, of elite politics.

Finally, the President and the politicians have not hesitated to delegate substantial power in economic policy formation, for they did not perceive the *técnicos* as a potential political threat. Since the administrators had no power base of their own, they have not been feared as political rivals. Indeed, until recently, the appellation "*técnico*" had the pejorative connotation of "mere technician," the tool of their political masters. This is in contrast with some countries, such as former colonies, where the politicians have hesitated to delegate power to the administrators, who appeared clearly as a rival elite.[30] In Brazil, paradoxically, administrators could assume roles of considerable influence precisely because they did not appear to possess autonomous power.

Because of these factors, particularly the distrust of private interests, the Presidents and the politicians have transferred much of their power in economic policy-making to the *técnicos*. Their power has been precisely *a function of the power of the politicians*, and has grown to the extent that the politicians neutralized pressures from the broader society, creating a situation of freedom in economic policy formation which could be transferred to the *técnicos*.

By the same token, the *técnicos* have had influence only within the framework of the President's power, and he has followed their proposals only insofar as they did not conflict with his own goals. As a clientelistic politician, however, the President has not usually had strong personal direction in economic policy, and he was usually oriented by elite opinion's judgment of the "objective needs" of the situation. Since the *técnicos* had a major role in formulating these perspectives, instances of divergence were rare. For, in addition to the factors tending to give power to the senior administrators in the day-to-day decision-making

---

[30] See Lucian W. Pye, *Politics, Personality, and Nation Building* (New Haven, Conn., 1963), pp. 115-117.

process, they also have a special place in long-term policy formation. The more prominent *técnicos* are also important nationalist ideologues and take a leading role in feeding into the political communications process their views on the country's economic problems. Hence they have the power that comes from conditioning the elite opinion within which the politicians and the President work. Both in choosing the policy issues that are raised and in delineating possible solutions, they influence the basic framework of ideas within which economic policy is approached.

THE *Técnicos* AND BRAZILIAN ECONOMIC POLICY-MAKING

The rise of the *técnicos* to a position of power in Brazilian economic policy formation has been an important element giving internal cohesion and stability to the decision-making process. As noted earlier, despite the succession of regimes and all the talk about political instability, the main lines of economic policy were reasonably constant since the late 1940's. Ideological stability and the constraints imposed by the chronic balance-of-payments problem have already been cited in this regard, but the presence of the *técnicos*—career administrators with similar views in the key posts of economic policy formulation—has also been a powerful contributing factor.

The prominent role of the *técnicos* in policy-making may also have raised the quality of Brazilian economic policy. As we saw in Chapter 6, with the notable exception of exports, government policy may in general have played a positive role in promoting Brazilian development. Much of the credit here must go to the *técnicos*.

This is not to say that Brazil was ruled by a group of all-wise technocrats. We have noted several instances where government administrators erred in their treatment of policy problems, and the *técnicos* themselves were responsible for the ill-conceived doctrines influencing some areas of Brazilian economic policy-making. The "technical" criteria evoked in the policy-making process were often permeated with ideology.[31] Although the

[31] The very importance of "technical" considerations and the deference they elicit have given rise to the phenomenon of the pseudo-technical study in Brazilian economic policy-making, and the use of "technical" criteria to justify ideological predispositions.

ideology itself contained elements of a rational model of economic development, these were not always made explicit and subjected to criticism. Moreover, the *técnicos* exercised their power only within the constraints of the political system described—in particular, of elite opinion and of the President's personal orientation. These could well lead to serious economic irrationalities.

I am suggesting only that the *técnicos* played a crucial role in dealing creatively with some of the difficult economic problems which Brazil encountered in the postwar period. Although errors were made, these should not overshadow the overall performance. In particular, having helped get the country into a situation of a rising real cost for imports, the *técnicos* were also able to cope effectively with some of the potential barriers to growth within *that* framework. At least until 1963, they were able, with the help of a dynamic private sector, to promote rapid development led by industrialization, and an aggregate growth record that few less-developed economies could emulate.

CHAPTER 9

Resource Allocation and Inflation

This chapter considers some of the implications of the Brazilian economic policy-making process for resource allocation. We will discuss some of the biases to which the system appears to lead, both as between the public and the private sectors and within the public-sector itself. We will also discuss the implications of this political system for central economic planning, and for the aggregate level of the commitments assumed by the policy-makers. This leads to a discussion of the political context of the Brazilian inflation.

The Policy-Making Process and Resource Allocation

The principal effect of the Brazilian government's extensive intervention in the economy has been to influence the *composition* of investment rather than the share of national income allocated to savings and investment. Despite numerous measures aimed at raising aggregate savings and investment rates, these showed no tendency to rise during the postwar period.[1] Hence the expanding government economic role led to a transfer, in relative terms, of investment resources toward the public sector and the projects it favors.

Given the nature of the policy-making process described, this can create a serious distortion in allocations. The sectors which the political elite consider vital receive the lion's share of resources, whereas other areas, where returns might be higher but which lack glamor for the policy-makers, may have their growth stunted. As noted earlier, government investment decisions often

[1] This is discussed in greater detail in my paper, "Marginal Savings Rates in The Development Process: The Brazilian Experience," *Economic Journal* (1968).

154

stemmed from an intuitive effort to overcome capital-market imperfections, and many economic infrastructure projects may indeed have been well conceived. But we should recognize the strong, potentially counterproductive bias built into such an allocation system if the prevailing economic ideology happens to be misguided, and if the sectors that do not rank high in elite opinion's priorities might contribute more to development than do the glamorous ones. Furthermore, the political dominance of the public sector also introduces a serious bias in that resources are directed to its activities even though returns might be higher in the private sector. This is, of course, the reverse of the distortion often encountered in capitalist countries.

This sort of system also imparts an important bias *within* the public sector's allocations. A system of clientelistic politics enables the government to deal with pressure groups mainly through marginal adjustments within its general allocation policies. Consequently, the policy-makers can allocate the bulk of their resources with a different political target in mind: elite opinion, which in the Brazilian case was oriented to the general goal of "development." As a result, much of government's investment may be directed to large projects which will impress "public opinion" with the President's development achievements. The contrast here is with the allocation criteria of a system where power is more widely dispersed: "a great policy of small services," to please individual pressure groups.[2] Thus allocation policy directed toward "public opinion" may lead to large irrigation dams or impressive highways, with less emphasis on distributing canals or feeder roads.

The effects of such allocational criteria on economic growth depend on specific conditions. Perhaps because of the importance of overcoming indivisibilities, or of mobilizing a greater volume of investment resources than would otherwise be possible, the "grandiose" approach may sometimes have greater promotional effects on development than a series of smaller projects. This need not always be the case, however, and many small, individually unimpressive projects (e.g., agricultural extension services) may not receive the policy support they deserve.

[2] Cf. Albert O. Hirschman, *Journeys Toward Progress* (New York, 1963), pp. 53, 55, 86, for a somewhat similar point.

This policy-making process also has implications concerning the possibilities for effective aggregate economic planning. The relatively weak political position of private-sector groups and their inability to resist government intervention does remove one major obstacle that exists in some capitalist countries. The major units within the public sector, however, can themselves stand in the way of effective coordination. The government ministries and the public corporations in such sectors as steel, petroleum, transportation, and investment banking have their own orientations. The fact that they are located within the public sector does not always make it easier to control their activities.[3] On the contrary, the *autarquías* and "mixed enterprises," with their own political base in elite opinion and usually with substantial budgetary autonomy, pose serious difficulties to efforts at coordination in a centrally conceived plan. Hence the problem of central control is shifted into the government itself, and the politics of planning in Brazil becomes a case of administrative and intragovernmental politics.[4]

Another important barrier to effective central planning is the difficulty Brazilian policy-makers have encountered in choosing among the many "necessary" allocations, and in setting priorities for public-sector commitments. The ideology discussed earlier did stress some areas for development and exclude others. The list of high priority sectors remaining, however, has still been very large in relation to public-sector resources.

This problem may appear conceptual, but it reflects some structural features of Brazilian politics. As noted in Chapter 3, most Brazilian allocation decisions were formulated within a *sectoral* problem approach, as key problem areas were identified and projects were formulated to deal with them. More generally, most Brazilian planning efforts have concentrated on sectoral planning.[5] In this process each approved sector—for example,

[3] For a description of similar conditions in Mexico, see Miguel Wionczek, "Incomplete Formal Planning: Mexico," in Everett E. Hagen (ed.), *Planning Economic Development* (Homewood, Ill., 1963), esp. pp. 178–181.
[4] Material on administrative and political aspects of Brazilian efforts at planning is presented in Robert Daland, *Brazilian Planning* (Chapel Hill, 1967), esp. Chapters 4 and 5.
[5] Macroplanning has been included in the form of projections of aggregate capital-output ratios, domestic savings, and foreign capital inflow. The ag-

roads, electricity, railways, and petroleum—received allocations according to the "needs" of its promising projects. However, any effort at ranking projects as *between* sectors according to their rates of return—which might be considered an essential part of aggregate economic planning—has been neglected.[6]

This failure to compare the returns from projects in one sector with the returns available from applying the same resources elsewhere may have been due, in part, to the fact that the concept of economic opportunity cost is not intuitively obvious.[7] Policy-makers may also be prone to adopt an unconstrained approach to budgeting if they have available seemingly unlimited "resources" from the Monetary Authority. What is noteworthy in the present context, however, is that the political system did not impose criteria of *political* opportunity cost on the policymakers. That is, they were not forced to consider within fairly narrow limits whether the payoff in terms of political support might not be increased by transferring resources from one sector to another. The contrast here is with political systems like the United States, where the policy-makers must consider the marginal political costs and returns of alternative allocation decisions.[8]

In part this reflects the Brazilian policy-makers' relatively strong political position compared with their counterparts in societies where the politicians have to make close calculations on political support. More generally, since there are no strong political parties that aggregate interests and mobilize voter support in favor of, or in opposition to, broad programmatic alternatives, the government has not had to consider that its commitments in

gregate projections, however, have not been related to the sectoral projects that form the core of the actual investment plan.

[6] To return to a parallel noted earlier: the Brazilian allocation process suggests important similarities with the budgeting for the military services in the United States defense establishment, at least in the pre-McNamara period.

[7] For example, P. J. D. Wiles has argued that Marxian economics even lacks the basic concept of scarcity, one of the conditions necessary for resource allocation on opportunity cost criteria. See his *The Political Economy of Communism* (Cambridge, Mass., 1962), pp. 50–56, 95.

[8] See Anthony Downs, *An Economic Theory of Democracy* (New York, 1957), a model which appears to correspond fairly closely with the realities of American politics in the 1950's.

one sector involved political costs and resources that might more profitably be employed for other uses. Because of its political autonomy and the absence of outside interest aggregation, it could approve without close discrimination many of the projects that were submitted, as long as they accorded with the dictates of elite opinion.[9] And precisely because this opinion is not segmented by class or pressure groups, *its* goals have been generalized "development," supporting *all* sectors favored by the prevailing ideology.

This feature has been much reinforced by a theme of Brazilian political culture that we have already noted—the tendency to focus on the *complementarity* of various (approved) sectors for the general goal of development, rather than on their competitive aspect. In such a framework, the various sectoral corporations do not press their claims on the President and elite opinion as alternatives competing for the same scarce resources.[10] Instead of such chipping away at each others' claims, *all* the projects of the sectors acclaimed as crucial for development are pressed directly upon the Presidency. Because of the lack of effective interest aggregation to sift and discard some claims before they reach this point in the policy-making process, it is hard to impose priorities and reject claims.

Because of the Brazilian political elite's support for generalized "development" and the absence of competitive interest aggregation and ensuing political opportunity costs to limit total commitments, the policy-makers' allocations could well reach a level greater than available resources. In the absence of any mechanisms to ensure balance between government commitments

[9] The total level of commitments has been subject to the constraint of some tolerable rate of inflation or its acceleration. The political context of the inflation is discussed in the next section.

[10] Such a focus, comparing the resources claimed by different participants does not appear to exist, either in some central allocating authority or between the different contending parties themselves. Indeed, in interviews, senior officials of various public-sector corporations were not aware of the magnitude of each other's claims on public resources, and when this was mentioned to them, they did not see them in competitive terms but affirmed that the country's development certainly also requires growth of capacity in the other areas. Choice and competition among areas appear to take place only *within* sectoral institutions. For example, the Development Bank chooses between its steel and its electricity projects; the Petrobrás between petroleum exploration and refining capacity.

and real resources, budget deficits with an inflationary impact could ensue.[11] Thus, coming together with these other features of Brazilian politics, the government's political autonomy could lead not to rational intersectoral allocations and effective central planning, but to the possibility for sustained inflation.

The Postwar Brazilian Inflation

During the postwar period, the annual rate of inflation in Brazil ranged between 10 and 20 percent through the 1950's, with acceleration to annual rates over 35 percent in the early 1960's. A notable aspect of this inflation was the extent to which it was sustained by government fiscal and monetary policies.[12] Part of the expanded public sector's investment and production activities was possible only because the government ran budget deficits in the creation and support of many public-sector corporations. The *autarquías* which elite opinion considered important for development were also given extensive access to bank credit. This process was made possible, in turn, by the *Banco do Brasil*'s ample rediscounting activities. The previous section suggested that the

[11] It should be noted that these features internal to the policy-making process which lead to inflation are conceptually distinct from the "sociological" theory of inflation. According to that theory, inflation is caused by socioeconomic groups putting forward demands which together exceed aggregate real national income. Such a process may well initiate inflation in some countries and may accelerate it, once started, in others. In the Brazilian case, however, the conditions of political structure on which we have focused were entirely capable on their own of generating large governmental deficits and relaxed monetary policy.

[12] Antônio Delfim Netto's regression analysis of the Brazilian inflation, with annual observations for the period 1945–1963, presented the following results:

$$\frac{P_t}{P_{t-1}} = 0.242 + 0.617 \frac{M_t}{M_{t-1}} + 0.159 \frac{C_t}{C_{t-1}} + 0.993 A_t$$

$$R^2 = .93$$

where P_t denotes the level of the general price index; M_t, the supply of money; C_t the cruzeiro cost of imports; and A_t, the acceleration of inflation, defined as $(P_{t-1} - P_{t-2})$. The growth of the money supply, in turn, was accounted for mainly by the deficits of the federal government. See Antônio Delfim Netto et al., *Aspectos da Inflação Brasileira e Suas Perspectivas para 1965* (São Paulo: Associação Nacional de Programação Econômica e Social, 1965), p. 29, p. 56.

Brazilian policy-making process may be inherently prone to assume commitments at a level higher than aggregate real resources. Let us now consider the specific features of the political context within which the issues of inflation and monetary stabilization were approached in Brazil during this period.

Any political unit which can determine the volume of its money supply has the potential for sustained inflation. The two possible constraints are (1) the availability of international credits to deal with the adverse balance-of-payments situation which inflation engenders and (2) the willingness of domestic political participants to accept continuing price rises.

Concerning the willingness to accept price rises, we should emphasize that, unlike some less-developed countries, Brazil's monetary tradition is not one of unquestioned orthodoxy and inexorable opposition to inflation. Rather, the prevailing doctrine has been that inflation promotes economic growth; and literally no important actor in Brazilian politics actually opposed the inflation. Established bankers, for example, who were the most vigorous opponents of currency depreciation in the United States in the nineteenth century, in Brazil generally have supported loose monetary policies. Having taken measures to protect themselves from capital losses, they believe that their profits are increased by the higher turnover which they feel inflation promotes. Business and industrial groups have also accepted the inflation, and have indeed been vociferous opponents of the restrictive money policies that accompanied the periodic efforts at monetary stabilization.

The political elite have also felt no strong commitment to price stability. First, the issue was posed in fairly special terms. It was never "inflation versus price stability," but rather "inflation and development versus price stability and economic stagnation." Although some economists have suggested that the choice between inflation and growth is actually a "false dilemma," neither the Brazilian *técnicos* nor the foreign experts they consulted have known how to stabilize prices without simultaneously restricting economic growth. The experience of Brazilian policymakers was that every episode in which monetary and fiscal policy were tightened resulted in a decline in growth. Moreover, Brazil has long been accustomed to some price rises, and the inflation did not appear to pose a threat of economic breakdown through runaway inflation. Since the value accorded economic development was much greater than the value placed on monetary stability, it is not surprising that the former priority prevailed.

Internal political pressures, then, have not been a barrier to inflation. The remaining potential constraint has been the balance-of-payments situation and, specifically, the willingness of international lenders to advance Brazil credits to deal with the international disequilibrium to which inflation led. In the postwar period these international lenders and the pressure to halt inflation in order to achieve balance-of-payments equilibrium have been personified in the International Monetary Fund. Under the postwar system of international relations, however, Brazil was always able to obtain sufficient international credits without actually stopping the inflation, and the periodic moves toward stabilization never went very far.

Apart from the other pressures cited, the question of monetary stabilization was given a very special interpretation within the political communications process. Price stabilization was conceptualized in terms of a setback to Brazil's thrust toward development of a modern economy. This connection was readily made, for only the unpleasant necessity of having to deal with the IMF seemed to stand in the way of the government's development efforts. Moreover, the international lenders and the pressures to disinflation appeared in the form of the IMF—a political body dominated by the advanced countries—rather than from commercial bankers or the less personal workings of the international gold standard. Consequently, the intelligentsia and the newspapers readily perceived an imperialist plot to maintain Brazil in the position of an agricultural export economy. This interpretation appeared amply justified because the IMF usually called for a devaluation and a consolidation of exchange-rates—the very demands of the coffee planters and the traditional export sector. Because the question of monetary stabilization was structured in terms of colonial dependence as against the drive for national economic (and political) emancipation, the full force of elite opinion was usually thrown against the anti-inflation efforts as soon as they appeared to restrict development.

Since neither the pressures for international equilibrium nor internal political forces acted to limit the inflation beyond the (changing) levels which elite opinion considered "tolerable," the policy-making process could generate the country's persistent inflation.[13]

[13] Some of the aspects of Brazilian economic policy-making—in particular, the absence of competitive politics and interest aggregation, and the political elite's commitment to generalized development—resemble features of the Communist countries. Why, then, was the development of the U.S.S.R., for example, not accompanied by inflation? The answer is that it *was*, albeit at rates lower than those of Brazil. The mitigating factors seem to have been (1) the existence of a strong central planning authority that made for a modicum of balance between aggregate demand and real resources and (2) the orthodox monetary tradition of the Soviet authorities. On these points, see J. Montias, "Inflation and Growth: The Experience of The Eastern European Countries," in W. Baer and I. Kerstenetzky (eds.), *Inflation and Growth in Latin America* (Homewood, Ill., 1964).

CHAPTER 10

The Slackening of Growth and
Prospects for the Future

In some of the earlier chapters we noted instances when Brazilian economic policy-making was ineffective because of the influence of faulty doctrine and analysis. In this chapter we will consider another example of this phenomenon, in the slowdown of Brazilian growth after 1962. Finally, we will discuss the sources of the informational weaknesses of Brazilian policy-making in some areas.

Economic Policy-Making in 1962–1964

After 1962 Brazilian economic growth slackened while the inflation accelerated to new and relatively high levels. Data on these developments are presented in Table 19.

TABLE 19. *Annual Percentage Change in Real GNP and in the Price Level in Brazil, 1960–1964*

Year	Real Output	The GNP Price Deflator
1960	6.7	26
1961	7.3	35
1962	5.4	49
1963	1.6	72
1964	3.1	91

Source. Fundação Getúlio Vargas.

Brazilian economic policy-making was unable to avoid these problems or to cope effectively with them. Coming together with a deep ideological and constitutional crisis, they contributed to a growing atmosphere of chaos which led to a military takeover in April 1964. Although the policy-making problems were compounded by the general political crisis, the government's failure to deal with the economic situation occurred because of the weaknesses of the previous decision-making process.[1]

ANALYTICAL AND TECHNICAL PROBLEMS

The slowdown in economic development appears to have been initiated by an import constraint; thus it resulted from the policies discriminating against exports. In the years before 1955 favorable quantum and price conditions in exports had enabled Brazilian imports to keep pace with the high rates of aggregate growth. As Table 20 indicates, however, after 1955 the supply of

TABLE 20. GNP and Imports, 1947–1964

Year	Indices (1954 = 100) GNP	Indices (1954 = 100) Imports	Annual Percentage Change GNP	Annual Percentage Change Imports
1947	67	49	8	40
1948	73	44	10	−10
1949	77	51	6	12
1950	81	63	5	22
1951	85	95	5	50
1952	90	92	6	−3
1953	93	70	3	−24
1954	100	100	8	43
1955	107	89	7	−11
1956	109	84	2	−6
1957	116	104	7	22
1958	124	102	7	−2
1959	133	113	7	10
1960	142	114	7	0
1961	152	106	7	−6
1962	161	99	5	−7
1963	164	102	2	2
1964	168	86	3	−16

Sources. Data on GNP are from Fundação Getúlio Vargas. Data on imports are from Conjuntura Econômica, index 117.

[1] As mentioned in the text, we are concerned here only with economic policy-making, and not with the general political crisis that affected Brazil

imports to the economy was almost stagnant. While GNP rose 61 percent between 1954 and 1962, imports did not increase at all. Furthermore, by the early 1960's, consumer goods had been almost entirely removed from the list of imports, which consisted mainly of raw materials, intermediate products, and capital goods. As the supply of inputs for the productive process failed to increase, a ceiling was placed on the economy's potential output.[2] Industrial output, which had been increasing at a long-term rate of 9 percent, was stagnant in 1963.

Brazilian policy-makers, however, failed to perceive the possibility of an import constraint on growth.[3] Rather, the general assumption was that the progress of import substitution, particularly in capital goods, had freed Brazilian development from dependence on foreign trade conditions. In fact, just as economic growth was slowing down because of income-inelastic supply of imports, the government's economic plan, authored by one of Brazil's leading *técnicos*, discussed the country's development prospects in the following optimistic terms:

> In the most recent period there has been an unmistakable acceleration in national economic growth, the annual rate having risen to 7% in the 1957/61 period as compared to 5.2% during the immediately preceding five-year period. . . .
>
> On reaching a phase of development where the process of capital formation leans mainly on our own production of equipment, the development of the Brazilian economy has come to depend on its own internal dynamics. Thus, no matter how important the external factors still may be, the rate of growth is determined mainly by . . . domestic market conditions. . . . A lag in external demand does not anymore, necessarily, result in a general slump in economic activity.[4]

in these years. Changes in the political context of economic policy-making are discussed below. As noted there, however, the informational deficiencies of the decision-making process were sufficient in themselves to lead to the unresolved problems of Brazilian development and economic policy.

[2] For a more detailed discussion see my paper, "Import Constraints and Development: Causes of the Recent Decline of Brazilian Economic Growth," *Review of Economics and Statistics* (November 1967).

[3] This seems to have been due to a lack of analytical clarity concerning the effects of import stringency and a failure to appreciate that it could retard growth as well as promote development based on import-substitution. See "Import Constraints and Development," Section IV.

[4] *Three-Year Plan for Economic and Social Development* [*Plano Trienal*] (Rio de Janeiro, December 1962), p. 18, pp. 25–26.

Not only was the slackening in growth not anticipated, but the policy-makers failed to deal with it when it arrived. First, diagnosis of the situation, which might have provided the basis for an effective policy response, was faulty. Indeed, the question of why growth was slowing down was rarely even asked; for the answer was taken for granted—the political crisis was believed to have caused a downturn in investment. Critical examination of this hypothesis was, in any case, difficult for anyone who wanted to undertake it, since the investment estimates for 1962–1964 were not available until late 1966.

The economic slowdown was also taken as evidence that development was being obstructed for lack of basic social, political, and economic reforms. There was almost no mention of anything so prosaic as income-inelastic supply of imports. These doctrinal interpretations did little to help policy-making. For example, the federal budget deficit was approximately 5 percent of GNP in these years, and with prices rising 1.5 to 2.5 percent monthly, there was ample evidence of excess demand in the economy. Nevertheless, some observers emphasized the need for changes in income distribution to provide an adequate internal market and avoid (Keynesian) stagnation! Similarly, although food and other agricultural production had, in fact, been rising satisfactorily during the 1950's and early 1960's, the country's economic slowdown was attributed to the lack of a land reform.[5] The share of imports in Brazilian GNP was as large as it had been in the early 1950's (partly because of depreciation in the real dollar/cruzeiro exchange rate). Nevertheless, it was suggested that "the

Year	Food Production		All Agriculture for Domestic Market	
	Index	Percentage Increase	Index	Percentage Increase
1960	100	—	100	—
1961	104.4	4.4	107.4	7.4
1962	110.2	5.5	115.6	7.6
1963	115.2	4.5	119.3	3.2

[5] The following figures from *Conjuntura Econômica*, indices 38–39, show the increase in Brazilian agricultural output in these years:

phase of growth based on import-substitution had inevitably reached its end" and that there was no longer scope for investment in import-substitution activities.[6]

Economic policy problems were further complicated by the acceleration of inflation. In 1962–1963, the government permitted large increases in the money supply. With domestic output constrained by the unavailability of imported raw materials and intermediate products, increases in aggregate demand now caused higher price rises than had been the case under previous, relatively elastic supply conditions. As a result of these conditions as well as the inflation's own internal dynamics—increasingly volatile expectations and more rapid wage adjustments—the rate of price increase reached new and unprecedented levels.

The acceleration of inflation added to the sense of chaos and loss of control, and at the same time it limited the government's room for maneuver in dealing with economic policy problems. With the annual rate of price increase exceeding 50 percent and posing the threat of hyperinflation, for the first time control of inflation was given a high priority. As mentioned earlier, however, neither Brazilian administrators nor foreign experts have been able to overcome the technical problem of how to stabilize prices without curtailing growth. A tight money policy implemented by Finance Minister Dantas in the second quarter of 1963 actually aggravated the recession because of its depressive effects in manufacturing and construction.

The economic situation in late 1963 and early 1964 also contributed to the confusion of the policy-makers by confronting them with a set of problems which they had previously not encountered. As noted earlier, the general belief had been that inflation was associated with growth. Now, however, on the one hand, inflation was accelerating, and at the same time growth was slackening. Such a conjuncture of events had not occurred before. On the contrary, the other economic slowdowns of the postwar period, in 1953 and 1956, had generally been interpreted as being due to anti-inflation policies, first under Oswaldo Aranha

---

[6] Clarification of the situation was not helped by the fact that many foreign observers were also overly rapid to accept some of these doctrinal interpretations. They are criticized on analytical and empirical grounds in my "Import Constraints and Development."

and then under Eugênio Gudin. (The connection had not been made between the previous decline in import supply and slow-down in production, which had led to an acceleration of the inflation and prompted these stabilization efforts.) This quick diagnosis of the earlier recessions had led to an equally clear prognosis of the appropriate policy to renew growth—looser monetary and fiscal policies. Such an approach had been all the more feasible in those episodes because the earlier deflation had reduced the rate of inflation and given greater scope for expansionary policies. Moreover, since in the meantime import supply had increased and loosened the constraint on production, the economy had been able to respond with elastic supply. In late 1963 and early 1964, however, conditions were very different. The situation of rapid inflation coupled with declining growth conflicted with previous experience and puzzled the policy-makers. The inability to cope with the new situation contributed to the sense of loss of control over the country's economic problems.

Even if the *técnicos* had been clearer about what to do, however, some important political changes had occurred which would have made the implementation of economic policy decisions more difficult.

Political Changes

In political terms, Brazilian economic policy-making in the previous period had two principal features. The political elite was clearly oriented in its choice of economic policy goals, and the government was able to concentrate sufficient political power to impose its decisions. After 1962, however, there were important changes in both respects.

As noted in Chapter 4, the early 1960's saw a shift in elite opinion, with a new emphasis on the need for "basic reforms." This contrasted with the previous concentration on economic development, without explicit focus on social and political changes. The movement seems to have been led by a change in the Presidency and by an ideological reassessment initiated by the intellectuals in the political communications process. But once it began, it took on its own dynamic, and previous leaders of the nationalist intelligentsia such as Hélio Jaguaribe and San Tiago Dantas soon found themselves far outflanked by more radical new positions.[7] And, although institutions such as the ISEB broadcast the new ideological positions to wider ranges of elite opinion, the ideas being fed into the political communications process changed so rapidly that only part of the political elite followed the movement. For others the shift was too swift and too radical.

This had two important consequences. First, the decisive orientation previously provided by the dominant economic ideology was lost, as there was no longer any clear structure of priorities between such goals as "basic reforms," economic development, curtailing the inflation, and reducing foreign influence. On the contrary, there was extensive self-questioning within the political elite concerning policy goals.[8] Indeed, policies which had previously been considered mutually consistent and indeed instrumentally linked, such as use of foreign capital to promote national economic development, or reliance on industrialization to promote a more democratic social order, were now seen as mutually contradictory. This confusion on goals was a problem which had previously not hampered Brazilian economic policy-making.

Equally important, the ideological consensus which had previously integrated Brazilian economic policy-making was shattered. For the first time in the postwar period there was no shared ideology whose authority facilitated the formulation and acceptance of policy decisions.[9] Some politicians had moved further with the radicalization of elite opinion than others; and within the movement's internal dynamic, as some politicians shifted to the left in support of major political changes, others reacted by moving to the right.[10] With this polarization in elite

[7] Cf. the distinction of Dantas and Jaguaribe between the "constructive left"—their own position—and the "negative left" of men like Brizola. See Jaguaribe, "The Dynamics of Brazilian Nationalism," in Claudio Veliz (ed.), *Obstacles to Change in Latin America* (London, 1965), pp. 179–180.
[8] Cf. the following description of the period, in "Fifteen Years of Economic Policy in Brazil," *Economic Bulletin for Latin America* (November 1964), p. 199: ". . . Never had such a welter of systems and measures been tried out and quickly shelved; never had discussions of economic policy been so much to the fore. . . ."
[9] Cf. the discussion of "Mobilization and Loss of Consensus" in Thomas E. Skidmore, *Politics in Brazil, 1930–1964: An Experiment in Democracy* (New York, 1967), pp. 253–256.
[10] The movement in elite opinion can be conceived as a changed frequency distribution, from a single-peaked one to a much greater dispersion at various points along the opinion spectrum.

opinion, the politicians were now split, and the President could
no longer mobilize support easily and indiscriminately, as previously, from a broad base among the professional politicians, including the center PSD as well as the more left PTB party.

Even so, a concentration of power sufficient to dominate the
situation and force policy decisions might well have been possible
if the President had been able to control his own forces. Among
the nationalist politicians, however, there was extensive conflict
on matters of personality, tactics, and policy. The new ideological positions had not yet crystallized sufficiently to provide
similar orientations. Moreover, no single leader within the group
commanded sufficient authority to provide cohesion and enable
them to act with their full power potential.[11] The President was
personally so inept he even lost partial control over his own political apparatus. As a result of these changes, whereas previously
major shifts in economic policy such as the vastly increased
public-sector role had been implemented so easily that they
passed almost unnoticed, the government now found it more
difficult to act in resolving policy problems.

Finally, economic policy-making was also affected by the
broader crisis that affected Brazilian politics. The call for "basic
reforms" carried the threat of profound shifts in the country's
power structure. Although many members of the political elite
went along with this movement, the military did not. With
their own communications system, they were far less open to the
compelling influence of the new ideas; and with their self-
conceived role as guardians of the national order, they feared the
changes that might result. At the same time, all propertied groups
came together to resist basic constitutional changes. Their efforts
at mobilizing broader opposition were also effective, for the middle strata too had failed to keep pace with the radicalization of
elite opinion.[12] This opposition of the military and part of the

---

[11] Cf. Skidmore, pp. 276–284, on "The Left: Divided and Over-Con-
fident." The President was so unable to impose himself as leader of the
"nationalist" group, and they were so little united, that, in the words of
one prominent member of the group, if the President and his major "lieu-
tenants" had all been given knives and left together in a dark room, the
result would have been mutual liquidation.
[12] The failure of all public opinion to make the complete adjustment to
the radical positions within elite opinion occurred for three reasons. First,

urban middle strata was to culminate with the deposition of President Goulart in April 1964. In the meantime, however, as the President was maneuvering for his political life, he showed little interest in economic policy, and resolution of policy decisions suffered.

These political changes would undoubtedly have made economic policy-making more difficult even if the analytical and technical problems of Brazilian growth had been overcome. To the extent that feedback did occur between the broad political crisis and the slowdown in Brazilian economic development, however, it went from technically poor policy-making, to the deteriorating economic situation, to a generalized feeling of loss of control and a need for political changes.

Our discussion has emphasized the intrinsic technical difficulties for policy-making—quite apart from the simultaneous crisis in other areas of Brazilian politics—once the *técnicos* had let the country reach the situation of an import constraint, slackening growth, and accelerating inflation. This interpretation is supported by the events following the military intervention. After April 1964, political power for effective decision-making *was* centralized, in the military government. The new regime also had an advantage which had been denied Goulart—substantial foreign credits. Nevertheless, policy-makers were unable to deal satisfactorily either with price stabilization or with the growth problem. The general price level rose 57 percent in 1965, while economic growth did not regain its previous momentum.[13]

the intelligentsia and the communications elite were connected with the international communications network to a much greater extent than the broader public and thus receiving messages from foreign media and international organizations. Working with a different picture of Brazilian economic policy-making than that presented above, the latter were constantly reiterating the position that Brazil needed "basic" policy reforms as well as "structural" political modifications to implement them. Moreover, unlike some smaller Latin American countries where political life is centralized almost exclusively in the metropolis, Brazil's regional capitals, especially São Paulo, still retain some independent political importance. In this shift in ideology and climate of opinion, although they moved very far, they did not keep pace with Rio de Janeiro. Finally, middle-strata opinion is formed by popular communications media which, unlike the "prestige papers" of the political elite and the intelligentsia, are more susceptible to the influence of interests opposing important political shifts.

[13] The rate of growth was 3.9 percent in 1965, but only because of exceptionally good harvests in agriculture. Industrial output *declined* as a re-

Prospects for the Future

Before concluding, it may be worthwhile to consider the prospects for economic policy-making in Brazilian development in the future. We can discuss this under two headings, the political context and the informational conditions underpinning decision-making.

It is probably too soon to assess the possibilities for Brazil to resume the previous political pattern, particularly after the impact of the two and one-half year military regime. The conditions underlying the system of clientelist politics have not changed greatly, however, so the major problem probably lies in achieving a new consensus orienting and integrating the political elite on economic policy issues.

If the actions of the post-Goulart regimes do not themselves increase dissensus, it may be possible to return to something approaching the previous ideology, with, as is being attempted, enforced exclusion of the nationalist dissidents. Alternatively, a new consensus, closer to the "extreme" nationalist position, may be in the process of formation. Such a process occurred in Brazil during the 1920's. Alienation of part of the intelligentsia and the political elite led to a decade of sporadic revolts against the older order, which could be supported only by martial law. The new ideas were unable to take effective political expression until, under the impact of the 1929 crisis, they were accepted in broader elite circles and, to avoid widespread national conflict, ratified by the military. That new ideology and consensus provided much of the basis for the country's achievements from the middle 1930's until the early 1960's.[14] Another possibility is that the experience and learning generated during the post-Goulart regimes will lead to the crystallization of new perspectives.

sult of the anti-inflationary fiscal and monetary policies. The year 1966 was also one of relatively slow growth.

[14] An important difference from the 1920's, of course, is the increased international involvement in Brazilian politics, which has added an important new dimension to internal conflicts.

THE INFORMATIONAL WEAKNESSES OF BRAZILIAN ECONOMIC
POLICY-MAKING

Over the longer term, however, the major problem for Brazilian economic policy may lie in the possibilities for correcting the informational weaknesses of the policy-making process. One aspect of this situation is the well-known absence or long delays in the availability of important statistical data for decision-making.[15] Perhaps even more important, however, is the poor quality of some of the technical analysis, exemplified in the unexamined (and sometimes erroneous) views that underlay some of Brazil's basic policy decisions. Despite the outstanding competence and the high quality work of many Brazilian economists, they were unable—as we have seen in this chapter and in our discussion of export policy—to influence the main current of the analysis affecting some key points of Brazilian development.[16]

The importance of accurate analysis for effective policy-making is obvious. I stress it only because students of development often have the intellectual's bias that the policy problems of economic development are preeminently *political:* give power to the right people, and they will know what to do. As we have seen, however, this is not necessarily the case. Even a modernizing political elite relatively free from political constraints cannot produce successful development policy if they are working with faulty perceptions and misconceived doctrines. Because of the importance of this problem for Brazilian development, let us therefore consider in greater detail why policy-makers have not

[15] A good example is the occasions when Brazilian policy-makers have been called upon to deal with "recessions" about whose very existence they could not base solid judgments because there were no statistics on employment of the labor force or utilization of plant capacity.

[16] It may be objected that I have been overly harsh in judging these aspects of Brazilian policy-making. Hindsight is always easier than current analysis, and some problems were inherently intractable on the basis of presently available technique. In this discussion, however, I am referring to the cases where major improvements could have been made with existing analytical techniques, and indeed an open mind would have been enough. The lags in perception of changing trends in world trade were too long by any standard, as was the persistence of doctrines that were ill-conceived even within the framework and goals of economic nationalism. On these points, see pp. 84–88.

always been able to draw upon more penetrating analysis of some of their country's economic problems.

The theme of the inadequate knowledge of their country's economic and social realities has long been raised by Brazilian writers. This "malaise" has usually been attributed to the intelligentsia's excessive participation in the intellectual world of Europe and the United States, and to the predilection for applying analysis and models "developed in the advanced countries, but totally irrelevant to a country at a different stage of development such as Brazil." [17]

Although the picture of the useless analyst, warped by his stay in Paris or Chicago, has a long tradition in Brazil, as in other Latin American countries, the percentage of Brazilian university students studying abroad has in fact been very low.[18] A larger proportion of the leading economists studied in foreign institutions, but this has not prevented many of them from becoming interpreters and practitioners of "nationalist" economics. In fact, as we noted in our discussion of protection, coffee valorization, and inflation, there are no grounds for charging the Brazilians with undue deference to laissez faire or to any other "imported orthodoxies." The theme of "cultural alienation," at least in economics, has been most relevant in Brazil mainly as a means for discrediting critics of the (strongly entrenched) indigenous interpretation of Brazilian reality.

It might appear that the analytical weaknesses of Brazilian policy-making and the substitution of doctrine for analysis are due solely to the ideology's stultifying effects on intellectual activity. What is "known" does not have to be researched, and beliefs with strong emotional support may clearly resist critical

[17] For a recent statement of this view, see Aníbal Pinto and Osvaldo Sunkel, "Latin American Economists in the United States," *Economic Development and Cultural Change* (October 1966). Cf. also Victor L. Urquidi, "Further Observations on Economic Research in Latin America," pp. 147–148 in Manuel Diégues Júnior and Bryce Wood (eds.) *Social Science in Latin America* (New York, 1967).

[18] In 1960, 0.7 percent of Brazil's university students were enrolled in overseas institutions. The percentage figures for Argentina, Mexico, Chile, and Colombia, respectively, were: 1.1; 1.3; 1.9; 4.4. For most African countries, the percentage ranged between 30 and 70 percent. These figures are given in Angus Maddison, *Foreign Skills and Technical Assistance in Economic Development* (Organization for Economic Cooperation and Development: Paris, 1965), p. 82.

questioning.[19] Even *within* the framework of economic nationalism, however, the *técnicos* made some important errors, notably
in the "exportable surplus" policy and in the "either/or" approach to the balance-of-payments problem, which lowered the
country's rate of aggregate growth *and* of industrial development.[20] Hence further discussion seems needed to explain the
poor quality of Brazilian economic policy analysis on some issues.

One ready answer is the lack of resources, principally well-
trained personnel, engaged in economic analysis in Brazil.[21] As
noted earlier, the Brazilian stock of highly educated manpower is
relatively low.[22] Hence the errors of some Brazilian economic
interpretation may be an indication of underinvestment in research, and a justification for increasing the number of qualified
economists, both in and out of the civil service. During the postwar period, however, there has been a very large expansion in
university-level teaching and research in economics. It is not
clear that the volume of useful analysis has risen proportionately.
Often the increase in numbers has led only to propagation of the
same myths, while research has frequently shown the same blind
spots as the prevalent doctrines. Topics for which the ideology
provided foregone conclusions have been neglected, regardless of
their importance for the country's development.[23] By the same
token, there has been little criticism or opening of new perspectives on major issues.[24] In light of this experience, more than an
increase in manpower and resources alone seems needed.

In particular, we should note some sociological aspects of eco-

---

[19] Such an interpretation, however, would underestimate the positive contributions the ideology has made in leading Brazilian analysts to consider
aspects of development which outside observers, with their different experience and perspective, would miss.

[20] See pp. 82–88.

[21] See, e.g., Urquidi, *op. cit.*, p. 146.

[22] See p. 97 (n. 18). In the present context, however, what would be
needed is not "high level manpower" (with university education), but people with advanced graduate training, enabling them to do independent
analysis.

[23] An exception to this lack of interest is some of ECLA's work. In addition
to its research on ideologically glamorous industries like steel and machine
tools, it has also studied more traditional—but important—activities such as
coffee and textiles.

[24] An indication of the influence of ideology on the climate of opinion
surrounding Brazilian economic analysis is provided in one of the few
studies of exports, Antônio Delfim Netto's work on coffee. Concluding an

nomic analysis in Brazil. First, as has often been noted, despite the outstanding performance of numerous individuals, economics as an institution has not yet been completely professionalized in Brazil. Partly because of the deficiencies of the universities, few of the higher level *técnicos* during this period passed through a socialization process in which objective standards for technical performance were internalized. In addition, some economists are not sufficiently differentiated from the general intelligentsia to operate in their professional roles on the basis of purely technical norms.

These problems are aggravated because Brazilian economists, and particularly the more competent people, assume many roles: they may often be simultaneously engaged in university teaching, the higher civil service, and business consulting. The most prominent may also on occasion serve as Finance or Planning Minister, and as ideologue and newspaper columnist as well. This pattern has much to recommend it for avoiding some of the negative features of overly "academic" work. It sometimes has its costs, however, in terms of the quality of the analysis performed. Quite apart from the magnitude of the pressures on key personnel, the different role requirements may conflict. Some issues may require a deeper analysis than is possible for people involved in day-to-day decision-making; and there may be a tension between rigorous technical work and political, administrative, and ideological needs.[25]

This problem also arises, of course, in advanced countries where economists move easily between research and policy-

analysis with suggestions for a more efficient coffee policy, the author makes the following defensive comment: "It would obviously be ridiculous to conclude that we are suggesting that Brazil should devote more attention to coffee and less attention to industrialization. Our position is that with a more thoughtful policy, we could have achieved the same development effort with lower costs; which is, in fact, more development." Antônio Delfim Netto, "Sugestões para uma Política Cafeeira," *Revista de Ciências Econômicas* (March 1962), p. 51 (n. 23).

[25] Florestan Fernandes seems to refer to the same problem, albeit with a different perspective: ". . . these [social] scientists, as a group, ultimately play a creative role in the dissimination of ideas, aspirations, and even myths which are very important for communities at a transitional state in the introduction of scientific technology." See his paper "The Social Sciences in Latin America," Manuel Diégues Júnior and Bryce Wood, *op. cit.*, p. 27.

making positions. Its severity is greater in Brazil, however, because professional standards are less institutionalized. Equally important, because of the greater scarcity of competent personnel, there are not enough people who remain outside the bureaucracy to continue more basic applied research and to maintain responsible criticism. As this indicates, this problem is partly one of numbers, but the importance of role differentiation and professionalization should also be stressed.

Finally, we should note another feature of Brazilian economic analysis: the absence of intellectual and institutional pluralism. During this period most of the resources for economic research in Brazil were concentrated in a single institution, the semiofficial Fundação Getúlio Vargas. This center made notable contributions to a deeper understanding of Brazilian development.[26] Because of its virtual monopoly, however, there was relatively little of the intellectual and institutional competition that might have stimulated criticism and innovation.[27] Studies of the sociology of science have indicated how important multi-centered intellectual structure, which permits and indeed promotes such rivalry, is for analytical progress.[28]

Some of the informational deficiencies of Brazilian policy-making are not surprising in view of the weakness of interest groups and political parties. As many observers have pointed out, one of the principal contributions of such groups in countries where they are strong is the provision of data and analysis for policy-making. Our discussion need not be interpreted, however,

[26] Because of inadequate resources, however, the Foundation had to devote most of its effort to compiling the national income accounts, so that relatively little could be done in way of analysis.

[27] Analysis by foreign scholars or by international agencies was accepted only insofar as it accorded with accepted doctrines.

[28] Joseph Ben-David and Awraham Zloczower, "Universities and Academic Systems in Modern Societies," *Archives Européennes de Sociologie*, III (1); Joseph Ben-David, "Scientific Productivity and Academic Organization in Nineteenth Century Medicine," *American Sociological Review*, XXV (2). Some of the other issues raised here—for example, the conditions for the formation of a commanding doctrinal "school" and the intrusion of orthodoxy in policy issues into professional development—are of course not unique to Brazil or to less-developed countries. For a discussion of these questions in a very different context, see A. W. Coats, "Sociological Aspects of British Economic Thought (ca. 1880-1930)," *The Journal of Political Economy* (October 1967).

to indicate that Brazilian economic policy-making requires stronger mediating organizations; for we can distinguish between the informational and the political functions of such structures. Information activities can be decentralized and organized along pluralistic lines even in a system where power is centralized. And if intermediate political structures were reinforced, Brazilian economic policy-making would lose one of its crucial positive features, its relative freedom from political constraints.

CHAPTER 11

Conclusions: Politics and Economic Development in Brazil

In this study we have considered the effects of Brazilian politics on economic policy formation and the country's economic development. For this purpose, we first discussed government action and the factors behind its decisions in four areas. Building upon these cases, we then formulated a general picture of the political system conditioning economic policy-making in Brazil. We can now summarize our conclusions on the interaction of politics and economic development in Brazil during the postwar period through 1964.

Politics and Economic Policy-Making in Brazil

The question of politics and economic policy-making in Brazil is raised against the background of views which have stressed the political system's inadequacy for effective economic policy-making. One view has emphasized the instability (in other areas) of Brazilian politics and cites anecdotes of gross irrationalities of the decision-making process. Another advances the familiar propositions that without basic political changes, either reformist or revolutionary, Brazil cannot expect to have a government promoting economic development. This picture portrays the political system as too dominated by reactionary coffee planters or *nouveaux riches* industrialists either to take a responsible attitude to popular needs or to formulate policies unconstrained by selfish interests.

Our discussion suggests, however, that the power of the *ancien régime* and of the coffee elite in national economic policy-

179

making has already been superseded. The government has, moreover, been operating in a political structure which insulates it in great measure from the partisan pressures of other groups, such as the industrialists, who might prevent the formulation or administration of policies impinging on their special interests. As we saw, the public sector could increase its share in national product by about 75 percent in the course of the postwar period. Two-thirds of this increase came from sharp rises in taxation which the government was politically able to implement, making the Brazilian public-sector's revenue share relatively high in comparison with that of other less-developed countries. The government also had the power to allocate these resources and others which it brought under its control—for example, imports and investment funds—in the ways it has seen best, with very little deference to vested economic interests or pressures from the private sector. Indeed, many scarce resources were appropriated for wholly new activities carried on in the public sector.

This autonomy in economic policy-making grew, as we noted, from a system of clientelistic politics which neutralizes many of the pressures from interest groups and socioeconomic classes.[1] Clientelist politics made possible policy action based on elite opinion, which in postwar Brazil followed a modernizing economic ideology. With the availability of the *técnicos*, in turn, these ideas could take effective programmatic form. These features of national economic policy-making which induced the political elite to take a modernizing approach and cope reasonably well with the country's economic problems are more than might have been expected from the conventional picture of politics and economic development in Brazil.

This is not to say that economic policy in Brazil is free from irrationalities. The President and elite opinion may introduce serious distortions of their own. Moreover, we have noted cases,

---

[1] As noted in Chapter 7, the military are an exception to the pattern of interest-group fragmentation through clientelistic politics. The military have been very important in Brazilian politics, however, mainly in other areas, principally as guardians of the national order. To the extent that they were involved in economic policy-making, this was in general support of economic development along the lines of the ideology: industrialization, modernization, and "basic industries."

principally export policy, where Brazilian economic policy was not well conceived from the viewpoint of promoting economic development. A policy-making system which is heavily influenced by ideology and "self-evident" truths is fortunate if these correspond roughly with objective reality. If they do not, it is useful if the assumptions of the policy-makers and of elite opinion can be made explicit and subjected to critical analysis. The ideology's powerful emotional supports may clearly pose a serious barrier here. Some features of this interpretation of Brazilian reality have appeared so "self-evident" that they have informed Brazilian economic analysis as axioms rather than vice versa. This situation exemplifies some of the difficulties for accurate economic analysis in a milieu where the economists are insufficiently differentiated from the intelligentsia and the intelligentsia hold strong ideological convictions.

We have noted certain aspects of economic research in Brazil that may account for the longevity of some of the unexamined—and sometimes erroneous—assumptions conditioning fundamental policy orientations. The point is, however, that these sources of possible irrationalities are *ideational* rather than political. The political constraints on Brazilian economic policy-making are much less binding than in a system where socioeconomic classes and interest groups exert a powerful influence on the decision-making process.[2]

Finally, in evaluating Brazilian economic policy-making, we should be clear about the standards used. In particular, many Brazilian or foreign observers appear to judge Brazil from a wholly unrealistic baseline.[3] If we bear in mind the blunders sometimes committed in the economic policy-making of the advanced countries, both socialist and capitalist, the Brazilian record does not seem poor in comparison.

[2] Because of this situation, the potential payoff from improved technical study of Brazil's economic problems is much higher than in countries where political pressures may more often prevent effective analysis from being implemented. Some of the analytical problems—for example, monetary
[3] In Brazil this seems to stem from a very idealized picture of economic policy-making in the advanced countries and particularly from the assumption that a higher educational level in the population leads to better-quality policy-making.

Economic Development and Politics in Brazil

We can also draw some conclusions on the political changes that have been associated with economic development in Brazil.

Brazilian industrialization dates from the last decades of the nineteenth century. With a growing internal market provided by the coffee boom, a substantial manufacturing sector developed on the basis of tariff protection, locational advantages, and the shift of relative prices between imports and domestic products coming from the persistent depreciation of the real exchange-rate. As a result of this industrial development, a new modern urban sector expanded and outflanked the older and previously dominant landed elites—particularly the export producers—depriving them of their former position in national politics.

A notable aspect of these changes is the extent to which they occurred gradually, without a once-and-for-all confrontation on the national level between the *ancien régime* and the new order. Actually, there were some issues of common interest, such as support for coffee to maintain the country's foreign-exchange receipts. More generally, major developments such as the extraordinary increase in the government's economic control occurred piecemeal, by the aggregation of many individual sectoral projects. In this context, the new situation in economic policy-making passed almost unnoticed. (Indeed, many observers continued to insist that for political reasons the government could not cope with the policy problems of economic development.) There has been no extensive violent struggle or a dramatic turning-point in the transition from the previous order that might approximate the conventional "revolution" or "reform" of ritual discussions.

This should not obscure the fact that although neither of these has come, important political change of a different sort has developed. Many aspects of the political change and of the present system may be distasteful—for example, clientelistic poli-

stabilization without economic retardation—are, of course, very difficult. This leads to the reverse of the position from which I personally started this study: namely, that the main problems of policy formulation for Brazilian development lay in political constraints, while the economic analysis and prescription were largely straightforward.

tics—and the changes have themselves led to new political and moral problems. This should not, however, divert attention from the fact that Brazilian politics are very different, with both new potentialities and new constraints, than they were a generation ago.

Our case studies indicated that the main beneficiary in economic policy-making has been the central government, principally the Presidency. This may appear surprising, for economic development has brought a new distribution of social and economic power and the emergence of new groups such as the industrialists and the labor unions. These developments might have been expected to limit government power and lead to more effective public participation in policy-making. The principal effect of the development of the new socioeconomic classes and the expanding middle sector, however, has been to dissolve previous political relationships and the power monopoly of the older elites. At the same time, decisive power has shifted not to the new groups but to the professional political class and the chief politician, the President.

In earlier chapters, we explained the politicians' dominance in terms of the historical conditions of Brazilian industrialization and the system of clientelist politics. In the pattern in which economic development came to Brazil, the bureaucracy and the professional politicians antedated the industrialists and labor groups and took control of the new groups through corporatist institutions such as *peleguismo*. The Brazilian government has even been able to control the financing and leadership of the Confederation of Industries; and interest groups have been reduced to dependence similar to the "company unions" which employers used to dominate the nascent labor movement in the United States.

This pattern has been reinforced by the system of patronage and machine politics, which have in great measure fragmented interest groups and socioeconomic classes and mitigated the impact of new groups' participation in politics. Another important aspect of economic development has been the government's greatly enlarged economic role, involving many new production and regulatory activities, especially the allocation of key resources such as foreign exchange and bank credit. The expansion of state intervention in the economy, coming without an extension of strong public participation in politics, further strengthened the political elite's ability to curb the influence of groups from the broader society. With the enormous increase in his carrot-and-stick patronage capacity, the President could create a central political machine, encompassing the politicians with local and regional political organizations, and dominating Brazilian politics. Hence, together with the weakening of previous power positions, economic development has led to greater centralization rather than diffusion of political power in Brazil.

The relatively meager influence that groups from the broader society have been able to exercise over the political elite and economic policy-making should not appear unusual. In terms of comparisons of economic development and political change in other countries, very few countries have followed the "classic" experience of nineteenth-century Britain or the United States, in which emerging socioeconomic groups were able to take control of the state machinery. Rather, the Brazilian case seems closer to what has been in fact the modal pattern, in which the politicians and the bureaucracy dominate groups such as the industrialists, and through manipulation of the power and economic resources of the state deprive them of much of their political potential. As the earlier reference to "company unions" in the United States reminds us, things can change, and political dependents can begin autonomous political activity. There are no clear signs of such an evolution now in Brazil, however, and even the events of 1962–1964 appear to have been brought about mainly by a crisis within the political elite itself.

Finally, we have also noted the importance of some features of Brazilian politics which are not always emphasized but which may be significant both for their general theoretical interest and for future empirical research. Among the important structural features noted was the model of clientelistic politics, which, it was suggested, may be more useful for conceptualizing Brazilian politics than the interest-group framework more commonly used. Another feature which clearly merits further study is the different "arenas" of Brazilian politics and their interaction.

We have also stressed the enormous importance of "public opinion." No detailed study of the Brazilian political communications process is now available. It would be especially interesting to have a clearer idea of its flows, and of the process by which issues are conceptualized. On some points elite opinion admits relatively rational formulations, whereas on others, as we have seen, it does not. Our study has also suggested the importance of a deeper understanding of the Brazilian intelligentsia, especially its internal interaction. The intelligentsia's consensus within nationalist ideology is particularly noteworthy since it was achieved without many of the political and economic mechanisms for centralized control used in other countries.

We have noted repeatedly the importance of Brazilian political culture, both in explicit formulations such as the modernizing nationalist ideology and in other pervasive attitudes such as the distrust of private groups and the preference for "technical" solutions. We have in addition underlined the importance of some political elites about whom relatively little systematic information is presently available, in particular, the professional politicians and the journalists. Finally, the prominence of the Presidency suggests the need for further research into the process by which Brazilian Presidents have been selected and on the exercise of Presidential power in policy-making.

Statistical Appendix

TABLE 21. *Export Taxation as a Percentage of Total Coffee Export Receipts*

(A)	(B)	(C)	(D)	(E)	(F)
			Cruzeiro Value of Coffee Exports Computed at the	*Cruzeiros Paid Coffee Exporters for their*	*"Exchange Confiscation": Coffee Export Tax as a*
	Dollar Value of Coffee Exports (millions	*Average Effective Import Exchange Rate (cruzeiros/*	*Average Effective Exchange Rate (billions of*	*Coffee (billions of*	*Percentage of Total Coffee Export Receipts*
Year	*of dollars)*	*dollar)*	*cruzeiros)*	*cruzeiros)*	*(D-E)/D*
1954	948	33.8	32.0	24.8	23%
1955	844	46.1	38.9	30.4	17
1956	1030	58.0	59.7	37.7	37
1957	846	58.1	49.2	32.9	33
1958	689	73.1	50.6	26.3	48
1959	733	117.3	86.0	50.1	42
1960	713	137.6	98.1	59.4	39
1961	710	205.1	145.6	78.8	46
1962	643	346.9	225.1	101.5	55
1963	747	526.1	393.0	186.4	53

Source. Data kindly made available by the Research Division of SUMOC. The average import exchange-rate (i.e., cruzeiro cost of all imports divided by their dollar value) includes the preferential *câmbio de custo* imports. So large a share of total imports entered this category, however, that during the period 1954–1960 the "preferential" rate averaged 78 percent of the average rate. This was computed from data supplied by SUMOC.

TABLE 22. *Government Profits on Coffee Exports as a Percentage of Total Coffee Export Value*

Year	Percent
1954	15
1955	6
1956	3
1957	14
1958	− 2
1959	−15
1960	−10
1961	− 2
1962	10
1963	31

Source. Data available from SUMOC on the value of coffee stocks which were purchased by the government but which could not be sold at desired prices were added to the cost figures in column *E* of Table 21. From these revised cost figures, the new profit percentage was computed.

TABLE 23. *Public Sector Expenditure as a Percentage of GNP, 1947–1960*

Year	Annual Percentage	Three-Year Moving-Average (percent)
1947	14.7	—
1948	15.3	15.7
1949	17.2	16.5
1950	17.0	17.5
1951	18.3	17.6
1952	17.6	18.6
1953	19.5	19.1
1954	20.2	19.6
1955	19.0	20.5
1956	22.3	21.8
1957	24.1	22.9
1958	25.0	25.5
1959	27.5	27.0
1960	28.5	—

Sources. Calculated from data supplied by the Center for Fiscal Studies, Fundação Getúlio Vargas. This material did not include data on the large expenditures involved in construction of Brasília. These were computed from material in "Gastos Públicos em Brasília," *Conjuntura Econômica* (December 1962).

TABLE 24. *Public Sector Taxation Revenue as a Percentage of GNP in Brazil, 1947–1960*

Year	Annual Percentage	Three-Year Moving-Average (percent)
1947	14.7	—
1948	15.3	15.3
1949	15.9	15.6
1950	15.7	16.4
1951	17.7	17.0
1952	17.6	17.4
1953	17.0	17.8
1954	18.8	17.7
1955	17.4	18.3
1956	18.8	18.5
1957	19.4	19.7
1958	21.9	21.1
1959	22.8	22.5
1960	22.9	—

Source. Computed from data supplied by the Center for Fiscal Studies, FGV.

TABLE 25. *Fixed Capital Formation as a Percentage of Total Public Sector Expenditure, 1947–1960*

Year	Annual Percentage	Three-Year Moving-Average (Percent)
1947	18.6	—
1948	24.5	22.9
1949	25.6	25.9
1950	27.5	25.0
1951	22.0	24.4
1952	23.6	21.7
1953	19.6	21.0
1954	19.9	19.2
1955	18.1	18.2
1956	16.5	19.7
1957	24.6	23.2
1958	28.5	26.8
1959	27.3	28.8
1960	30.7	—

Sources. Computed from data in *Revista Brasileira de Economia* (March 1962); "Gastos Públicos em Brasília," *Conjuntura Econômica* (December 1962), and material supplied by the Center for Fiscal Studies, FGV.

Index

Abbink Mission, 46
Adhemar de Barros, 118
Administrators, *see Técnicos*
Aggregate demand, *see* Demand, aggregate
Agriculture, 12, 39, 46, 58, 80, 90, 96, 139, 141, 161, 166
Allocation decisions, 2, 3, 95, 97, 98, 117, 156
pattern of, 43-45
Allocation policy, 35-58, 93, 120, 143, 155
Allocation of resources, 35-58, 95, 140, 154-159, 180, 183
domestic, 36-40
imported, 40-43
Almeida, Salvio de, 100n
Analysis, economic, 173-178, 181
Aranha, Osvaldo, 99n, 167
"Arenas," 98-99, 126, 184
Argentina, 92, 137
Armed service ministries, 124, *see also* Military
Autarquías, 156, 159
Automotive industry, 47-48, 52, 65
Autonomy, 4, 19, 33, 57, 68, 73, 74, 77, 84, 100, 101, 109-131, 134, 144, 156, 158, 159, 180

Baer, Werner, 11n, 17n, 30n, 33n, 59n, 75n, 77n, 78n, 79n, 80n, 90n, 93n, 95n
Balance of payments, 3, 14-19, 29, 34, 47, 49, 55, 60, 62, 66, 68, 72, 73, 77, 78, 80-81, 83, 86, 91, 94, 99-100, 101, 105-106, 137, 141, 149, 152, 160, 161, 175

Banco do Brasil, 4, 35, 37, 55, 97, 111, 116, 117, 144, 146, 159
Banfield, Edwin C., 119, 120n, 123, 126n, 135n
Baran, Paul, 104n
Barbosa, Rui, 10
Bargaining, 64, 114-115, *see also* Autonomy
"Basic industries," 39, 45-48, 51, 53, 56, 58, 62, 93, 97, 102, 140, 148
Bello, José Maria, 5n
Ben-David, Joseph, 177n
Bonilla, Frank, 71n, 110n, 117n, 142n, 143n
Branco, Castello, 27
Brasília, 39, 45, 49, 50, 54, 126, 135
Brazilian Institute for Democratic Action (IBAD), 115
Bureaucracy, 26, 50, 80-81, 96-97, 100, 132-133, 143-153, *see also* Civil Service
Business elite, *see* Industrialists

CACEX (Carteira de Comércio Exterior), 81
Calógeras, J. Pandiá, 23n, 33n
Campos, Roberto, 147
Capital, 104-105
Capital flow, 60, 72, 75, 93
Capital, foreign, *see* Foreign capital
Capital formation, 37-39, 42, 45, 49, 52, 57, 75, 92, 93, 94
Capital goods, 19, 54, 55, 56, 60, 165
Capital-Output ratio, 93-94, 156n
Cardoso, Fernando Henrique, 109n, 114n, 115n